CW00727795

And the talk slid north, and the talk slid south,
With the sliding puffs from the hookah-mouth.
Four things greater than all things are,
Women and Horses and Power and War.
Ballad of the King's Jest. Rudyard Kipling

Author Deborah Bragg has been an advertising copywriter, magazine journalist, newspaper features editor, flying instructor with her own flying school, and college lecturer. And, as a complete novice herself, Deborah once trained a Shire horse called Bella.

There is no doubt in her mind which of all those things gave her the biggest problems and the greatest satisfaction. This is her story — and Bella's.

GREATER THAN ALL THINGS

TRAINING BELLA THE SHIRE HORSE

Deborah Bragg

© Deborah Bragg 1998

ISBN 0 9527638 5 0

The rights of D Bragg as author of this work have been asserted by her in accordance with the Copyright, Designs and Patents Act, 1993.

All rights reserved. No part of this publication may be reproduced, stored in a retrieval system, or transmitted in any form or by any means, electronic, mechanical, photocopying, recording or otherwise, without the prior permission of the author and publisher.

British Library Cataloguing in Publication Data:
a catalogue record for this book is available from the British Library.

For Chloe,
with all my love

Designed, printed and bound by MFP Design & Print
Stretford, Manchester M32 0JT. 0161 864 4540.

Published by FIDO PUBLISHING
Nether Hoff, Appleby-in-Westmorland CA16 6BD. e-mail fido@thorburnicus.demon.co.uk

INTRODUCTION

I am not a horsey person, by any stretch of the imagination. Just five years ago you'd have seen me turn tail at the sight of horses in my path; and I always gave them as wide a berth as possible. By and large horses left me completely cold; only two kinds ever stirred my blood – cart horses and racehorses – and then only from a safe distance. It seems to me that both represent a magnificent combination of grace and power. You might wonder how a heavily built carthorse could ever be graceful, but then you can never have seen the magical sight of a Shire at full gallop, tail held high, head and mane tossing and muscles rippling rhythmically.

Although I had a pony-mad daughter, nothing would ever have induced me to be so foolish as to sit on a horse, and what I knew about the species would fit on the proverbial postage stamp.

And yet despite my complete lack of horse sense (or common-sense, some might argue) I found myself breaking in my own young Shire horse. I say 'found myself' because I don't know quite how I got into this extraordinary situation. I suppose whereas some are content simply to admire these superb animals from afar, I wanted one of my own, and then I wanted to work one which led to breaking.

It took me two years, and during that time I kept a record of our progress, not with the thought of publication, but so that I would be able to recall the great steps forward, rather like a mother records first tooth, first step, first word and so on.

Although this is Bella's tale, the story really begins in May 1987 when my husband Q gave me the most fabulous birthday present ever: a massive carthorse called Friday. I had fallen in love with him at first sight, but Q seemed adamant that we didn't need, didn't want and couldn't

1

afford him. Imagine then my surprise and delight when I saw Q walking Friday down our long drive. Friday was eight years old and unbroken. I had no thought then of working a heavy horse, I was content simply to love him and amble round the marshes with him. Nobody could have loved a horse more. So I was devastated when he died in November 1988 after escaping from his field and devouring half a bucket of chicken mash. I had no intention of ever getting another heavy horse: Friday had been so different, so very special, so Friday. But like devils on my shoulder, people kept muttering about it being a waste of all I'd learned etc. etc.

And so along came Bella – and this diary. It's a story of appalling mistakes – bred from ignorance and inexperience – and genuinely horsey people will cringe with horror. It's a story of ten steps forward and twenty back, of hopes, fears, battles and victories. This is emphatically not a guide to breaking a Shire horse; more a cautionary tale of how not to do it.

Truly it has been two years of blood, sweat, tears. . . and Bella.

Main Cast of Characters

Stanmar Lady Anne, the heroine of the story, born 24 April 1987, registered Shire Number 143223, bred by Stan Hammond

Chloe, my daughter (born 1982)

Q, my husband who gave me my first Shire horse

Diane Seeley, who came to me as a cleaning lady and ended up as an invaluable assistant with horse breaking knowledge stretching back a lifetime, but no previous experience of carthorses

Mark Pell, farrier of extraordinary patience and courage, who I suspect now wishes he'd never been recommended to me

Crispin Clark, renowned horse vet, loathed by Bella who tries to flatten him at every opportunity but his determination is greater than Bella's

Martini, Chloe's 13.2 Welsh cob mare

William and Humphrey, the donkeys

Wilbur and Orville - Gordon Setter/Retriever crosses - and Sam, a Springer Spaniel

GLOSSARY

Frog	fleshy, central part of the foot acting as a shock absorber
Hitch cart	a pair of wheels and an axle with a seat on top, and shafts or a pole - perfect for the lazy and unfit!
Liverpool bit	a straight bit with an adjustable curb chain, mostly used in traffic
Long-reining	driving a horse on two long reins attached to the bit to teach discipline and rein aids
Lunge	the first schooling lesson where the horse is taught to circle round the trainer by means of a 30 foot long rein attached to the halter
Mud fever	sore condition of the fetlocks and heels, usually caused by standing in mud
Roller	leather band round the girth
Surcingle	stretchy band round the girth
Thrush	an infection in the foot caused by dung or mud
Top and bottom latches	Leather thongs or straps to secure hames round the collar at the top and bottom
Trace harness	harness used when one horse goes in front of the shaft horse to help him pull a heavy load
Trolley	four wheeled cart
Tumbril	two wheeled cart

Author long reigning Bella

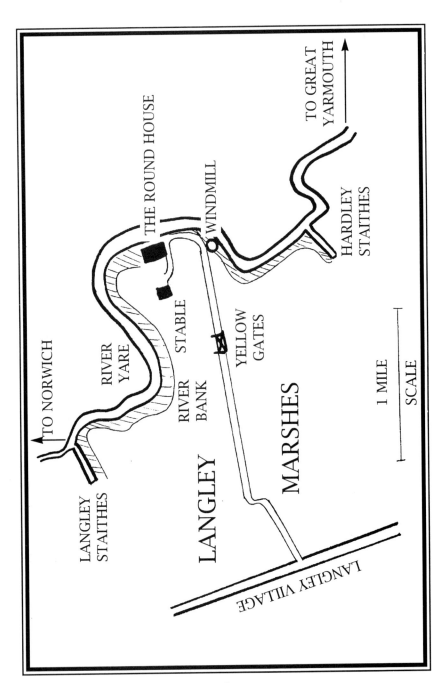

TO NORWICH

LANGLEY
STAITHES

RIVER
YARE

THE ROUND HOUSE

WINDMILL

STABLE

RIVER
BANK

LANGLEY

YELLOW
GATES

MARSHES

TO GREAT
YARMOUTH

HARDLEY
STAITHES

LANGLEY VILLAGE

1 MILE

SCALE

January 21st

We went to Norwich market and brought a strikingly glamorous cockerel and some hens. We were late home for lunch, and while it cooked I savoured wine and the Eastern Daily Press. "Shire horse filly with four white feet," I read. It was so unusual to see a Shire advertised in the local paper that I persuaded Q to ring. "£800" the man said, "and not quite two years old." After a couple of moments' deliberation, I rang back and said we'd be there in two hours. I didn't really want to take the restraining hand of Q but I'd had far too much to drink to drive myself, so Diane came too to balance things out. We finally found the place: an isolated farm deep in the fens, surrounded by endless dead straight dykes and roads. A spare man with a face that looked as though it had weathered half a century of the cruel fen blows came out of the house and introduced himself as Stan Hammond, followed by his daughter Bridget and her husband Norman. It had been Bridget's job, apparently, to wash and groom the filly in preparation for our arrival. The Hammonds led us to a large barn which housed perhaps eight Shire horses. It wasn't clear at first which was for sale, but Chloe marched straight up to one and announced, "I like this one – can we have it?" It turned out that unerringly she had picked the filly. We looked her all round, without any idea of what we were looking for, but there and then I agreed to have her: Stanmar Lady Anne, or Annie for short. If I'm honest I think the decision to have her was made when I read the paper: seeing her was merely a formality.

January 22nd

I had a sleepless night. Am I doing the right thing? Is it too soon after Friday? Am I going to live to regret such a mad-cap, drunken decision? Q reassures me that it will be OK, but I am still worried! I have always been impulsive – some would say headstrong – and it has frequently got me into trouble.

JANUARY 28TH

Her Ladyship arrived! The Hammonds backed their lorry into the top of the drive and let down the ramp – but Annie refused to move. We tried cajoling, handfuls of fresh grass, all manner of gentle persuasion, but to no avail. All four spotless white feet remained glued to the lorry floor. She looked out at the rain sweeping across the sodden marshes and decided, quite understandably, that she'd like to go home to her mum. So Diane and Stan Hammond got in the lorry and pushed, while Bridget, Norman and I pulled and then, just when we had almost given up, she burst out. Diane set off down the drive while I settled up and followed in the car. We had decided that it would be kinder to walk the filly, rather than subject her to a bone-shaking lorry ride over the numerous potholes in what Q grandly calls "our drive". (The fact that postmen, dustmen, oil tankers and numerous friends without the benefit of tractors refuse to attempt it perhaps gives a more accurate picture of the two mile approach to our lonely house!) It took them 45 minutes, giving me ample time to reject the Hammonds' pet name of Annie (connotations of my dumpy, grumpy grandmother perhaps?) and decide on Bella. Bella for a beautiful black body and four flashy white feet. The walk down the drive was an experience in itself, but the fun hadn't even started.

Bella emphatically did not want to go into her stable. The three stables were in existence when we bought the house, and were clearly built for normal-sized horses.

Certainly they must have seemed very cramped to Bella in comparison to the spacious barn she had just left. We tried going in forwards, sideways and backwards; quietly, patiently and noisily. After an hour in the rain of trying to convince her that it was really very welcoming in there, it was tempting to ignore Stan's advice about keeping her shut in for a few days. But we persevered and finally she backed herself in. Diane and I closed the door in soaked relief while Q fetched a bottle of champagne. Never before has champagne tasted so good.

FEBRUARY 2ND

Horror of horrors, Bella has gone lame. Crispin came and found she had an abscess deep inside one of her feet. Luckily Q was home because it certainly needed the three of us to battle with her. Poor Bella. In pain, a new home and a strange man apparently intent on torturing her. She reared, she lashed out, she tried to flatten us against the wall. Her eyes were wide with terror and I suspect ours were too. After two hours, Crispin gave up and hoped he'd cut away enough. "You'll have to clean out and spray it twice a day for at least a week," he said. I looked at him, shell shocked. How?

Crispin looked at me over the top of his half-moon spectacles and chuckled "I'm sure you'll find a way, Debbie."

FEBRUARY 3RD

I rang Diane in desperation, and the two of us tried to deal with Bella's foot and failed. Used to dealing with bulls, Diane is a pretty solid person – but she was no match for Bella's great foot. And I was completely useless. So in the evening her husband David came too. David, a farmworker, is much younger than Diane, knows nothing about horses, and yet he bravely held the foot while Diane held her head and I cleaned and squirted Terramycin. What a palaver.

"For £800 I'd sell this horse and give in," I declared in frustration. Diane and David looked at me in amazement, but with some sympathy and understanding too.

FEBRUARY 6TH

Four days have passed since Crispin said to keep Bella in for a week. But she had other ideas. By the time I got home this afternoon she was out and the frame of her stable door was lying on the concrete. Let's hope Crispin was being over-cautious with his seven days.

FEBRUARY 27TH

It was a beautiful bright morning, and so we walked Bella, who seems to be quite recovered, the whole way up the drive. She was silly at first, stopping and slipping in the mud, but she soon settled down and walked as quietly as Friday used to. On the way back she got hot, itchy and very very tired, so tired in fact that she couldn't even make her front legs walk straight, they kept crossing over!

Our lonely marshland home must seem reassuringly similar to the fens where Bella was born. I fell in love with the place instantly. The house itself is unremarkable; like a child's drawing, it is square with a door in the middle and symmetrically placed windows with a steeply pitched pan-tiled roof and central chimney stack – but its position is unique. Two miles from the nearest neighbours and just feet from the river. Like the fens, the flat surrounding marshes stretch endlessly into the distance.

It's nice to see that Bella is growing very attached to

Two year old Stanmar Lady Anne surveys her new companions with something akin to disbelief

William and Humphrey, whereas they seem to regard her with mild curiosity but mostly disinterest. The other day, William took hold of Bella's halter and led her towards the gate. I wished I'd had my camera!

MARCH 1ST

It is said that there is nothing to break the wind that blows here straight from Siberia and today I could verify that statement. It was bitterly cold and blowing hard, and Diane and I felt it would be folly to risk Bella playing up in the wind, especially after she'd been so good on Monday. So we groomed her and picked out each foot. She was superb! I was delighted – and relieved.

MARCH 20TH

Mark came to do Bella's feet. This was the big test. Would she behave like I'm sure she always did before the abscess – or play up? She was fine on the front feet – even the one that had given us all the trouble – but she certainly decided to test Mark with the back ones. Mark hung on for grim death as her leg pistoned back and forth. He apologized in advance for any bad language if he fell over, but I told him I'd be relieved to hear any language, the worst thing would be silence! But he won in the end and hopefully Bella will realize that he means her no harm. Watching Mark today, sweat pouring down his agonised face, I wondered at any farrier who chooses to work with heavy horses. I found Mark because I asked top farrier and judge Richard Gowing to recommend somebody. Mark was immensely flattered - it is a great accolade apparently – and so keeps coming. Young and fit with a cheerful disposition he is the ideal farrier for what can only be described as a difficult client.

Bella I mean, not me!

MARCH 21ST

Busy start to the day with one of the lambs apparently missing. I couldn't believe it. How could a lamb vanish? Then I heard a newborn cry from the other side of the wall of their shelter, and so I looked round and saw a lamb just making its debut. I then realised I could hear three lambs crying but could only see two. I finally found the lost lamb wedged firmly between the partitions. I extricated him with enormous difficulty, but his mum seemed less than thrilled to see him. Perhaps she had stuffed him in the corner! I checked on the lamb next door, only to find that yet another had appeared. I'm so glad my sheep just get on with the job, rather than requiring any inadequate midwifery skills from me.

Diane and I decided to take Bella on the river bank rather than up the drive as a tractor was filling up some of the many holes. Diane seemed very nervous but Bella was impeccable. It's strange: as my confidence in Bella grows, Diane's seems to diminish. I hope mine isn't misplaced.

APRIL 1ST

Some April Fool! For the first time I walked Bella alone. I took her along the river bank after first ensuring Q shut the gate behind me and watched in case I got into difficulties. With a dyke one side and the river the other, I felt confident she couldn't go anywhere if I did inadvertently let go. Outbound she walked surprisingly well, not so fast as she had with Diane, but she kept on snorting – I presume with excitement, which alarmed me somewhat. The steady chugging of the cruisers didn't seem to worry her at all, but we could have done without the flapping sail of a yacht going about. Coming back we were not quite so controlled as she insisted on trying to walk on the same blades of grass as me. We were only out for 10 minutes, but it felt more like 10 hours, and my right arm is definitely two inches longer.

APRIL 12TH

I don't believe this. Bella seemed to be having difficulty putting one of her back feet down so I called Diane and she diagnosed mud fever. When we applied Protocon we discovered she had the beginnings of it in the other three feet as well. I feel most indignant. The book says that mud fever comes from being forced to stand in mud or dirty bedding and shouldn't occur in a horse that is properly looked after. Bella does not have a wet or muddy field (and she doesn't have to stand in the small amount of mud that there is), and her stable is immaculate. What a little madam she is! It'll be lovely when we can actually start working this horse rather than simply treating her.

APRIL 19TH

Mike (my cleaning lady's husband) came to dig the garden today, and so I asked him to hold Bella while I did her feet. He looked a bit alarmed at the prospect - especially since she's in season and terribly randy with any men - but she behaved beautifully. I really must get her used to being tied up so that I can manage her feet alone. I don't mind the front ones but she does tend to wave the back ones at me.

APRIL 26TH

A superb Spring morning – at long last, after a week of endless rain. I groomed Bella until she shone and gleamed like satin. For the first time I tied her up. She didn't seem to mind at all – has she been tied up before or was she just being good? Her mud fever seems to be getting better. I now have this lurid green stuff from Crispin. Each time I feed her, morning and night, I lift her feet and pour it on. She's now the only black Shire with four green and white feet! Maggie at Chloe's riding school told me that white feet are much more prone to mud fever than black, something to do with the pigment, apparently. I am learning all the time.

APRIL 29TH

Chloe and I went to the first Eastern Counties Heavy Horse Association auction. There were piles of harness – some very dilapidated – carts, hames, harrows, ploughs as well as a few more mundane items like lawn mowers and jigsaws. I saw Paul Heiney, and at the risk of being thought some ghastly television groupie I went and introduced myself as the person who had contacted him last year with a view to picking his brain on working horses. He was politely distant, but I ventured to ask his opinion on the harrows. He suggested one or two that would be suitable for a single horse. I then studied the piles of harness, had a sneaky look in my book of harness to figure out what they were, and found myself not a lot wiser. I felt I couldn't bother Heiney again and so I decided to bid for a saddle and breeching and hope for the best. How I hate auctions! I'm never sure whether the auctioneer is looking at me or somebody behind me, and it's even worse when you're not 100 per cent sure what you're bidding for! Anyway, I got the harrows for a tenner, a saddle and breeching for £24 and a bridle for £5. I thought then that I ought to call it a day so I paid, loaded the harness into the car and went to pick up the harrow. To my chagrin I found I couldn't even lift the pole, and it was obvious now that it was much longer than I'd realised, certainly a lot longer than my car. Then I spotted David Wones' low loader and asked if he'd help. He kindly agreed so I stayed until he was ready to go; a delay that led me to buying some genuine old horse brasses for £16. I felt very pleased with the day. Chloe had been exceptionally good playing on a set of tyres for hours, so we celebrated with beefburgers and chips on the way home.

May 3rd

Diane came today and together we picked out Bella's feet. She's got a touch of thrush and so I must get some Stockholm tar which Diane says will help. We came to the conclusion that it will always take two of us to do her feet. I simply cannot hold on with one hand, leaving a spare to pick out or treat. We put a surcingle on her and she took it surprisingly well. Diane suggests that I try it on her at regular intervals and then turn her loose in it, before we try the roller. After picking out her feet and putting an elastic band round her tummy, it seemed only fair to give her some pleasure. And so we walked to the yellow gate. She was lovely. Obviously she's still young and silly but I feel sure that basically she has a kind, gentle, willing nature. Already she shows signs of being anxious to please.

May 15th

First day on the working heavy horse course at Otley College. When I saw this course advertised some weeks ago I immediately rang up, only to be told that all six places were already allocated. But it so happens that I know Keith Broomer, head of agriculture, who very kindly agreed that I could sit in as an observer. Anyway, I'm delighted because I learnt a lot today – even little things like feeding limestone flour with Equivite to strengthen the bones. Roger and Cheryl Clark are running the course and Cheryl is adamant that I must break Bella this summer or it will be too late. "She must never find out that she's stronger than you," she warned me darkly.

MAY 16TH

Today we covered harness: what everything is and how to put it on. If only I could have had today's knowledge before I went to the auction. I could have bought so much more if only I'd known what it was – and cheaply too. I've also found out that Paul Heiney's advice on my harrows was completely incorrect; they're not what I need at all. Chloe topped my horsey day by cantering alone for the first time. She said to me afterwards, "It's awfully bouncy, isn't it?" and I had to admit that I had absolutely no idea!

MAY 17TH

The best day of the course so far. Today we were under the tutelage of Roger and Cheryl. What a team they make! The Clarks are leading experts in showing and working heavy horses, and I was a bit worried about making a complete prat of myself. I'd imagined Cheryl would be very intolerant of people who made mistakes and harsh with the horses after what I'd heard of her breaking techniques, but in fact she is remarkably nice and patient with us and even kinder with the horses. Roger is the quieter, more thoughtful of the pair with a terrific understated sense of humour.

Cheryl, on the other hand, talks non-stop with the loudest and most infectious chortle I've ever heard. Obstreperous horses have broken countless bones causing her to walk with a pronounced limp, but her face is still as unlined as it must have been in her teens. I learnt so much today from them both, although the more I learn the more I realise what a daunting task lies ahead. Six hundred pounds to have Bella broken by Cheryl is beginning to seem a very tempting bargain. We spent the day hitching two tolerant Percherons to a tumbril and trolley and driving them round an obstacle course. Will I ever remember the harnessing up order: T chain near side, T chain offside, breeching off side, breeching near side, wanty (that's Suffolk for the belly band or strap that goes underneath to stop the cart going up if the horse rears). I learnt that lifting up shafts of a tumbril is nearly impossible for a single handed woman, so Bella must be trained to back between raised as well as lowered shafts. In the evening Roger talked about footcare and shoeing. Earlier in the day he'd mentioned that some horses are ticklish about the feet and that instead of lifting by the feather, one should pull up the heel and hang on to the toe. "It will immobilise them," he said with conviction. I honestly couldn't see how holding Bella by one toe would immobilise her, but when I got home I tried it – and it worked! Roger also said that he thought Bella had heel bug rather than mud fever – the two apparently look very similar - and he gave me lots of old-fashioned recipes like pig oil and sulphur for keeping wetness out of hairy legs; Fullers earth and lead acetate for grease and mud fever; zinc sulphate and lead acetate for heel bug; meths and a cooling lotion for sore shoulders; copper sulphate for thrush. Best quote of today I think was Roger's "Forget all that crap about these horses being gentle giants. They're not. They're lethal machines." Would I have done better to buy a mynah bird?

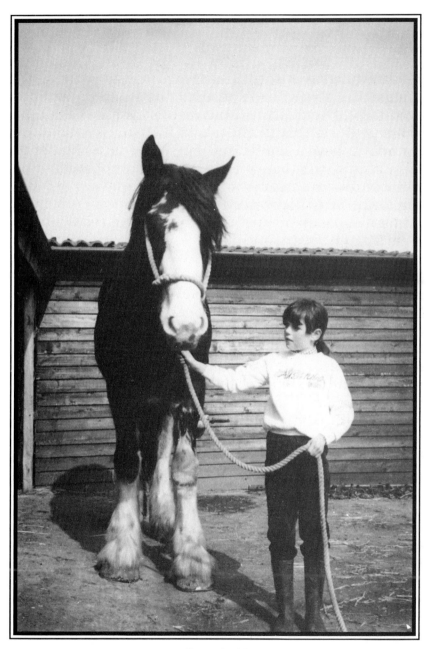

Bella and Chloe

MAY 18TH

Most of today was spent practising harnessing up to the four wheel trolley and the tumbril. We also practised painstakingly our knots – much to Cheryl's amusement. Then the treat of the week: we took Sam in the tumbril and Noble in the trolley out on the road. We all agreed that this was definitely the life: ambling along country lanes, lined with cow parsley and blossoms, under a blue sky and May sun to the distinctive clip clop of heavy hooves.

MAY 19TH

Last day of the course and the others are all getting nervous about their tests. I left them to it and went to work for a couple of hours. As a finale Roger showed us how to plough and roll – back-breaking stuff but satisfying. In one day a man and two horses can plough an acre; in the process of so doing he will walk 11 miles. So the average field around here of eight acres would take more than a week to plough. What a relief the invention of the tractor must have been. (To date the fastest recorded time in a tractor for ploughing one acre is nine minutes 49.88 seconds). It's all very well for us to wax lyrical about the "good old days" picturing horses and carts meandering home in the dusk, laden with corn. The reality must have been frustration, exhaustion, the hell of seeing a harvest ruined by the weather and the constant battle for survival. But in defence of the horse, the tractor damages the land by compaction and in a lot of cases can't go where four legs can. The Clarks know the arguments for and against horses because they work their 117 Suffolk acres solely by horsepower.

I wonder what kind of people the College and the Clarks

expected on the course – it was the first heavy horse course the college had organised. Not, I suspect, the mixed bag that they got. Interestingly, I was the only one who actually owned a heavy horse. Jenny (who with tumbling dark hair looked just Hardy's Tess when she was driving the tumbril) ran a garden centre and had intended to buy a pair of heavy horses at the end of the year. After the course she wasn't quite so sure. John will be working Suffolks at Hollesley Bay where I'm sure he will cause havoc with his perpetual lusting after large women! Barry was the joker of the pack, into carriage driving and hoping to set up an equestrian centre. I suspect he'll never buy a heavy horse; used as he is to thoroughbreds, he found the Percherons' slow, steady stroll very frustrating. Carol, shy and diffident, is a groom at a riding school. Tom already has sheep, pigs and ponies, with a Percheron filly arriving soon. Dean, the youngest, was probably the most knowledgeable of us all about horses. Cheryl regarded us all with a kind of tolerant amusement but she seemed pleased that we all tried so hard. It was an excellent week and I believe that everyone with a heavy horse should go on a course like that. Preferably before they buy the horse!

MAY 24TH

A gloriously hot day – again. Can this heatwave last? Diane and I took Bella off the river bank – away from her beloved William and Humphrey – and put a bridle on her for the first time. We opened up Friday's old bridle and then I eased open her mouth and put the bit in. She mouthed it like mad but I suppose you would, wouldn't you, if someone put a bar of cold metal in your mouth. But she didn't seem unduly fussed. Next was the roller. It obviously felt much thicker and less giving than the surcingle, so she arched her back like a cat and pranced a little. But after a few minutes she relaxed and so we walked her to the pump house. "No further?" she seemed to ask as we turned her round. "No", said Diane, "or you'll get jaw ache."

After Diane had gone I called round to John Wones about a breaking cart. John is a young lad who works for his Dad's garage. He got hooked on heavy horses through old Gilbert Edwards (who sold us Friday) and now has two Shire geldings. I think he's beginning to realise that my interest in heavy horses is not the flash in the pan he thought it was. It is difficult to convince some of these Norfolk boys that I am serious – just because I don't look the part.

John said he could make a breaking cart using our old axle but reckoned I'd be wasting my money. He goes straight from sledge to tumbril. He then asked how I was getting on for harness and I said, it's funny you should mention that but please could I borrow a couple of collars to try for size. To my surprise he readily agreed and so I set off with two, and met Diane on the way home. I held Bella with the halter while Diane gently eased the larger of the two collars over her head. It seemed to my untutored eye a tight squeeze but Bella stood quietly and didn't seem at all bothered about the dead weight on her shoulders. It's a good fit to start with but I know I shall have to buy one, if not two more collars, as Bella grows.

MAY 25TH

John agreed to sell me the 23 inch collar for £40. So now I have a full set of harness: John's collar, the saddle and breeching from the auction, and hames that a local farmer unearthed in his barn .

MAY 26TH

While waiting for Mark, I endeavoured to put Bella's bridle on. Not a success. I frightened her badly and failed to get the bridle done up. I hope I haven't put her off. I will have to try again tomorrow with Q's help. It's not easy doing these things alone. Even if Q was interested in helping - which he isn't - he is so rarely here. The original phantom husband!

MAY 27TH

My birthday. Sad to think that it was just two years ago that Q walked Friday down the drive and into my life. What a horse he was. Even now, there's a lump in my throat and tears in my eyes when I remember seeing him at the end, head hanging miserably down, his whole body shivering and wracked with pain. Crispin came out twice that night but he couldn't save him. I shall never forget the horror as I stumbled in the dark wet morning over his massive inert body. He was stretched out just as he always lay when fast asleep - so much so that for a moment or two I didn't really believe he was dead. Now, whenever I see Bella or the donkeys lying like that, I feel compelled to call them, to wake them to reassure myself that they are all right. There will never be another Friday.

Together Q and I tried to get the bridle on Bella but failed again. I would never have believed a horse could keep its mouth so tightly shut or hold its head so high. We gave up rather than put her off for good, but it was disappointing. And so to console myself and mollify her (or should that be the other way round?) I walked her to the yellow gate. She walked like a lamb apart from the occasional head down to get a munch of grass. When I yanked her halter to stop her, she tossed her head high with a petulance that seemed to say, "All right, if you won't let me eat I'll pull your arm right out of its socket."

June 1st

Mummy came to stay and just four miles from Loddon, her exhaust fell off. I took her up to the Wones' garage who I knew would fix it quickly and reasonably. When we went to collect the car, John offered to show me his sledge. It's a most interesting contraption – not exactly eye-catching but perfect for the job. Just a few planks of wood bolted together, with steel runners to help it move easily. Ideal for breaking and then for shifting harrows, a plough, straw etc. around on. I shall take Q up to look at it so that hopefully he can copy it.

June 7th

After quite a struggle Diane and I succeeded in getting the bridle on. She quite understood how I had failed single-handed. We also dressed Bella in the collar and the roller and again she was amazingly receptive. She is beginning to look like a real working horse!

June 8th

Diane was due to come but after I had brushed Bella until she gleamed, picked up her feet and put on the roller, there was still no sight of her. So rather than wait with a fidgety Bella we set off down the drive and met Diane half way along. Bella was being angelic, plodding along like a real old trooper so we kept going, past the bullocks and on

Bella poses in bridle, collar and roller

to the road. Oh, the sight of Bella – with her ears pricked as high as they would go and her eyeballs out on stalks. What was that strange clip-clop sound? that washing waving on the line? that dustbin bag? We only walked a short way and luckily didn't meet anything untoward, but Bella had obviously enjoyed herself. Her sulkiness on the way back was evident.

Later Mark came and she behaved appallingly. Who would be a farrier? Mark hung on while she dragged us both around, and incredibly, never lost his temper. He smacked her once, quite deservedly, and when she went all huffy, his tone was soft, "You are a big baby." He is worried about her back feet. Are they so narrow because she's young? He admits he doesn't know and I certainly don't. William was impeccable and Humphrey was such a pain in the neck that he escaped altogether.

JUNE 18TH

One of the joys of owning animals is coming back to them from holiday. Others dread going home, but I love it. First stop was the kennels where the dogs nearly bowled us over. Wilbur is hoarse having howled non-stop and Sam has kennel cough. Orville, laid-back as always, simply smells kennely. When we finally got home it was round to see the rest of the zoo. Diane has obviously done a lovely job – everybody looks hale and hearty. Bella seemed a little wary – has she forgotten me so quickly?

JUNE 28TH

Diane is tied up with the Norfolk Show this week, and the Royal the next, so I decided I must take Bella out on my own. While we were away Diane admitted that she hasn't done anything with her, so it's been some time since she's been out. And it showed! I gave up half way to the yellow gate as she kept stopping and looking wild-eyed. If only it would stop raining and we could get the hay in, we could start lungeing her in the field. The river bank really is no good for that sort of thing.

JULY 12TH

What a long time since we've done anything. Diane and I took a very reluctant Bella out, but a touch of the whip on her tummy soon got her moving on. All the bullocks were near the fence and Bella was frightened, but we kept her going. We took her on to the road and again she was amazed at everything she saw. I think if you'd said boo to her, she would have run for home! We're now so relaxed on the drive that Diane and I chatter constantly behind Bella's back, about sex, husbands, children and all the usual topics women natter about. And it's obvious that Bella listens – because the minute we stop talking her ears start to waggle uneasily back and forth until we start again.

JULY 15TH

Friends came for a barbeque lunch as it was such a gorgeous day. Unfortunately the barbeque fell to pieces so Q had to hurriedly build one out of bricks. We'd only just finished eating when Stan Hammond and his family arrived to see Bella. I think they were impressed. Stan seemed surprised that she was so big, and on the subject of battling with her back feet he suggests a blindfold might be worth a try. I do hope they stay in touch, they're a lovely family.

July 18th

Diane is away on shows, so I decided to put Bella's bridle on by myself. After six attempts, I finally succeeded, only to lose the top strap and have the bit fall out! But I eventually won and then I walked her up the drive, complete with whip.

July 20th

Bella bit Q. I don't know what happened – and probably never will. Q says he was just mucking out her stable and she suddenly lunged at him and bit him on the arm. Certainly he has a livid bruise but I cannot believe Bella would bite unprovoked. Kick, maybe, but not bite.

July 22nd

Having managed the bridle twice on my own, today I failed. She jerked her head up and broke the rope. I decided to give up with the bridle and instead made her stand with the roller on while I picked up each foot in turn. No problem. I also put zinc and castor oil on her blistering nose. I noticed that Bella has become paranoid about the wheelbarrow. I wonder if she frightened Q by cornering him in the stable and he drove the barrow at her? There has to be some reason why she bit him.

July 24th

Chloe and I went to the West Runton Shire Horse Centre which was very interesting. David Bakewell talked about harness and heavy horses in general and then dressed one of the Shires in harness for a few minutes' harrowing work. He has a lovely collection of old implements but it's sad to see them in a museum when Bella and I could be using them. Chloe loved the gypsy caravan and longs for us to have one for Bella! I talked to David about breaking Bella and he suggested the best way was to put on all her harness and then leave her tied up for a week. I'm sure there are people who do that, but there has to be a kinder, gentler way. It's interesting to note that David hasn't broken any of his horses himself. I'm rapidly learning that most people I meet have their horses broken professionally – but that doesn't stop them advising me on how to do it!

Chloe joined the other children for a waggon ride, and I was really shocked to see David load all the children in before he climbed in himself at the rear – with no one holding the horse's head. Roger and Cheryl's words about safety have obviously made an impression on me.

July 26th

A major milestone today! We lunged Bella for the first time. At first we tried it as the books suggest: with me on the outside of Bella, but Diane was worried that I would be trampled and so I stood to one side and left her to get on with it. Bella was extraordinarily good – certainly much better than Friday was on his first attempt. She didn't like the whip, but Diane gently stroked her all over with it to show that it didn't hurt. At one point, Bella worked herself into a terrific paddy, stamping her feet and backing up to Diane, but on the whole it went very well. The combination of biting flies and high humidity can't have helped.

Diane lunges Bella

July 28th

Mark came, and to our surprise Bella was much better behaved. However, Mark is worried about one of the back feet again, but for a different reason, – a bad case of thrush, he thinks. I rang Crispin who suggested one part hydrogen peroxide to 10 parts water as a scrubbing solution and spraying with Terramycin and antibiotics. Neither he nor Mark seem to favour Stockholm tar for thrush. Crispin is very generous about giving free advice on the phone – although his wife always sounds somewhat guarded and protective of him.

July 30th

Q bought a rubber-wheeled trolley for £100. John Wones is going to collect it and replace one of the tyres. I haven't seen it yet, so I hope it's the right size and weight. We shall need a separate barn for horse-drawn implements at this rate.

July 31st

Bella is going really well on the lunge now and we have started long-reining her too, using the commands "wheesh" for right and "come here" for left. I may not have a traditional East Anglian horse but at least I'm using the correct regional commands! We were so pleased with her, but she rather undid the good work by lashing out when we tried to scrub and spray her foot afterwards. She's been so good about it the last two times, but she's obviously learning fast. After I nearly lost my front teeth, we decided to enlist David's help in the evening. Between the three of us and a sheet wrapped round the leg, we finally managed it with aching backs as the only injuries.

August 2nd

Bella learned two things today: that she is allowed to trot on the lunge (but only when told to) and also to long-rein off the bit. "She's going just dandy," says Diane.

August 3rd

We put Bella's collar on again today and she raised no obvious objections – but refused to come out of her stable. I thought she looked dozy and had decided not to do any work today, but Diane said she was bewildered. Funny to think that it's only four months ago that we were begging her to go into the stable! Anyway she moved all right when I went behind her and told her to get out in no uncertain terms. Tonight, she was much better having her foot done. We really do have it down to a fine art. I hold Bella's head (the relatively safe end), David holds her leg up with a twisted sheet while Diane scrubs and sprays. The hydrogen peroxide bubbled up nicely tonight – probably because I strengthened the solution – and Diane reckoned it didn't smell any more. By the time I come back from holiday, let's hope I have a beautifully lungeing, long-reining horse with four healthy feet. At least I know she's in good hands while I'm away.

August 14th

A week of concentrated effort by Diane and the results are really showing. Bella is going well on the lunge and long-rein although she still has an unnerving tendency of backing into you sometimes. We tried both driving bridles on today. The one that I bought at the Watton sale doesn't seem to fit at all, but the other will do fine although the leather is very hard and stiff. We tried them on in the stable and Bella was very tolerant, although she held her head high and eyed us uneasily.

AUGUST 16TH

Today we dressed Bella in all her finery for the first time – collar, saddle and breeching, which resulted in her bucking, rearing and nearly mowing us down. Twice the breeching came off, but we put it back on – and then she refused to move at all. "She's in a state of shock," Diane decided. So we gently coaxed her forward until she walked round calmly and reasonably steadily. After such frenetic activity, the breeching is in need of a few stitches.

AUGUST 17TH

I finally found R Miles, harness maker and saddler in Framlingham. A delicious smell of leather in his little shop by the castle. He's going to mend and tidy up the saddle and breeching and make a top latch for the hames so that we don't have to use baler twine. "You must be from Norfolk," he said, "Down here in Suffolk the top latch is always a strap buckled round, while in Norfolk it's a leather thong." He loaned me a 24 inch collar to try, but it was too narrow to go over Bella's head which is disappointing as it's a nice one and reasonable, at £100.

AUGUST 22ND

Bella is getting increasingly difficult to catch and halter. She watches carefully as we go into the tack room. If we come out with the halter she's off and yet when she sees the box of brushes she visibly relaxes and stands as good as gold. She's even got wise to us hiding the halter behind our backs. Today we lunged and long-reined her in the driving bridle. What a shock to the system! I walked all round her, touching her gently and talking to her to reassure her that although she couldn't see me she was not alone. By the end of 20 minutes or so Bella was beginning to settle and accept her blinkered world. From now on, it'll be driving bridle only.

AUGUST 30TH

A great sense of achievement today – I lunged Bella alone for the first time. On the whole she was very good although I did have a few problems making her stop to my whoas. I didn't long-rein her as I still don't feel very comfortable confronted by that huge backside. (Will I ever?)

AUGUST 31ST

Diane thinks that Bella needs a complete break from lungeing and long-reining, despite the fact that she arrived to see Bella performing beautifully for me on the lunge. I simply cannot see how we will ever progress if we stop and start all over again – and told her so. I fully appreciate Diane's exasperation and Bella's boredom with the same dreary old lessons. But surely, I argued, the answer is to move on and add variety to the training. Finally I convinced her and so rather against her probably better judgement, she has agreed to come tomorrow. Tonight Bella and I had a long talk in the dusk. As I scratched her forelock and persuaded her that she has got to try harder, her eyes closed in blissful contentment.

SEPTEMBER 1ST

Bella obviously took in her lecture last night. We dressed her in collar with hames, roller and bridle and took her out for a walk round one of the fields. She behaved beautifully. Then we tried out the plough band and hitched up one side of the whipple tree. Despite the jangling and fiddling about, Bella stood dozing patiently in the sun. The whipple tree looked far too close to her hocks so over coffee we searched through pictures to check whether we had got the right equipment in the right place. We're still not really sure. There seem to be so many variations in harness – some regional, some according to individual idiosyncrasies, that it's really very difficult to know what's right. "Oh, it's all so trial and error," sighed Diane but at least today Bella inspired her not to give up. In the afternoon Sam and Wilbur found an injured greylag goose on the marsh. I carried her home, but I don't expect she'll make it. She's only been shot in the wing, but they usually die of shock. The marshes round here are all let for shooting, but it seems to me that many of the guns aren't true sportsmen. I've seen some shooting without dogs, others even so despicable as to target ducks sitting on the water. Shooting duck, geese, pheasants must be fair game on both sides.

SEPTEMBER 2ND

Q took Chloe riding, so I decided to play with Bella. I caught her with no problems at all (contrary little devil that she is) and put on the bridle and lunged her for just a few minutes each way. Enough, I hope, to remind her of her lessons and not too much to get her bored. She was lovely. Then I walked her up the drive and round a different field. She walked well, interested in the ducks that fly up under her nose but under control, and I think she enjoyed it. I felt so confident this morning that I would like to try long-reining her tomorrow. Dare I? (The goose is still alive but she is having difficulty moving).

SEPTEMBER 3RD

I dared! I didn't do any work in the field, but having put on roller, bridle and long reins, I took her straight on to the drive. Q held her while I sorted out the reins and whip and then we set off. She went superbly. I was so excited and exhilarated. It was tempting to keep on but I wanted to quit while the going was good so I turned her in a stubble field half way up to the yellow gate. There was a split second when she was faced with a huge open field that I could have lost her, but I turned her steadily back on to the drive, and the moment was gone. Pony nuts for Bella and a glass of wine for me – well done both of us!

SEPTEMBER 4TH

Variety is the spice of breaking! Today I put roller, collar, hames and bridle on Bella. It's the first time I've done it all alone, and it's certainly not easy, but with the help of a bale and a lot of patience from Bella I managed. She wouldn't come out from under the stable canopy at first, and she looked as though she was going to lie down at one point, but eventually I persuaded her that there was plenty of room, and no she wouldn't hit anything. We walked well, in-hand, up the drive.

SEPTEMBER 5TH

Diane arrived with back-up in the form of David. First she led Bella round the field with David and me pulling on the traces to give the impression of weight from her collar, and dragging a girder behind us for sound effects. Then we attached the whipple tree and chains to the back band with lunge lines, one of us on each side and Diane at the head before attaching the girder to the whipple tree. Finally we tied the chains to the back band with baler twine and Diane long-reined her while I walked silently just behind her shoulder with a third line to her halter. If she had taken off, Diane could have let go of the off-side rein and between the two of us we could have brought Bella into an ever decreasing circle. At least that was the theory! But to Diane's amazement, Bella was really good and apart from the odd shy and jump, coped very well with such a new and exciting experience. Certainly Diane seems happier although I sense underneath she would like to give up. But having spent so much money, I am determined that she sees us through to the end. To leave us at this stage would be grossly unfair, and I don't think Diane's conscience would allow her. But her reluctance is obvious. I do understand her apprehension – Bella is very much bigger, heavier and more powerful than the ponies she's used to breaking. When we first met she was desperate for cash, which was why she was working as a cleaner. But now she's beginning to get a few ponies in for breaking, and I think she'd like to dump Bella and me for an easier life. Things have been tough for her with little money and single-handedly bringing up two boys before she met David, so I can't really blame her for wanting to opt out.

The greylag goose has died.

SEPTEMBER 7TH

Another first for me and Bella. It was a glorious hot sunny morning (how long can this heavenly summer last?), and so I decided to wash Bella's feathers. She eyed warily the bucket of Lux flakes, but apart from flinching at the first splash, she accepted it quite calmly. For this first attempt I used Q's car washing brush, but I think next time I'll use a scrubbing brush. I dried each leg with a towel, and then let her go, to dry in the sun. It was a good experience for both of us and I shall try to do it regularly.

I had a long chat with neighbouring farmer Roger Loades this afternoon. Amongst many other topics we covered was the last working horse they had on the farm. "We used to love it when Father went to market. We'd get the hoss – a Suffolk Punch she was – all harnessed up and some of us'd ride her and the others would lead her. She never hurt a fly, that hoss. Father said she'd stay where she'd always worked until she died. She was over 35 when she died, down in the pit. The man with the lorry said he couldn't risk getting bogged down and couldn't we drag her out by tractor. Father was furious. "If she can't go with dignity, then she's not going anywhere," he said. Eventually they got the lorry down to her. There was nearly a world war that day over that hoss." I remember Roger's father: a big, patriarchal old man with the broadest Norfolk accent I ever heard. I probably missed some fabulous stories because I couldn't understand half of what he said – and I didn't like to keep asking him to repeat it.

SEPTEMBER 11TH

Diane arrived with David and it was a delight to discover that Bella's new 26 inch collar fits a treat. (I saw it advertised in the EDP along with other heavy horse harness, but because I was working I missed most of the stuff.) Q collected the collar for me on Sunday from a John Wiggins for £80. We did good work today with Bella dragging the girder round the field.

SEPTEMBER 12TH

First time pulling for just me, Diane and Bella, but apart from a couple of mishaps (like when the quick release knot released at the wrong moment) we three girls did well. As a reward, we long-reined her up the drive afterwards.

SEPTEMBER 16TH

I lunged Bella today for a change. She was not good. Her circle was somewhat ragged and she didn't want to keep trotting. A lesson to me that the basics must be kept up. I spent a long time soaping and waxing all the harness, including the saddle and breeching which I collected yesterday. For £58 it is all in one piece again. Q knocked out the back wall of the stables in readiness for Des Rolfe who is going to come and build them up in time for the winter. Winter is definitely on the way: today I heard their haunting cry before I spotted the first flock of wild geese heralding the coming of my favourite season here. The usual comment from first-time visitors here is: "It must be lovely in the summer." They never understand why I love it best in the winter. I revel in the bleak desolation, when the freezing rain drives horizontally across the marshes, blotting out all signs of civilisation, and penetrating every layer of clothing.

Diane works Bella — wrong harness but it is getting her used to the feel of the saddle and breeching

SEPTEMBER 18TH

A great example today of how easily accidents can happen to the ignorant. Diane couldn't come and so, rather than waste a crisp sunny September morning, I decided to lunge Bella alone. Because the back wall of the stables is down, I decided to tie Bella to the trailer reasoning that as it was full of rubble it was as solid as anything. I had just finished brushing her when something startled her. Up went her head and off went the trailer. As the trailer moved she panicked and would have made off completely if I hadn't been able to get hold of the rope and calm her down. If I had been in the tack room she would have gone, her terror increasing as she dragged the trailer with her. I was lucky. The lesson is: always use quick release knots tied to loops of string so that the string breaks first. As it was, it took me ages to undo the knot tightened by Bella's panic. Despite such near disaster I was still itching to try the saddle and so, foolishly really, I decided to put it on but without the breeching. I tucked the loose straps under the girth. She moved forward very reluctantly – it obviously felt very strange. I lunged her fairly well, sometimes having to stop and push the saddle back up, but I decided trotting was not on today! Then I walked her up to the pump house - no further as she was acting decidedly strange: head high, ears back, eyes wild. It's incredible to think that just a few months ago I thought I was very daring just walking her on the river bank. Am I completely potty?

SEPTEMBER 22ND

Three steps forward, two steps back. Today was not one of our better days. For the second time this week we dressed Bella in full harness and she still hasn't accepted it. To make her trot on the lunge, Diane hung on with both hands, while I ran behind cracking the whip. Long-reining wasn't much better, although it has to be said it is a magnificent sight when a ton of horseflesh rears! Finally, we long-reined her up the drive and she was so exhausted by this time that she walked with no problems. However, her strength and determination had returned by the time Mark came to do her feet. Three feet no problem – but that troublesome back foot lashed out at Mark with horrifying venom. Eventually we tied her to the gatepost and I stuffed apples in her mouth in the vain hope of distracting her from the task in hand while Mark finally won the battle.

Unfortunately the trouble has not cleared: there are now maggots in the deep clefts either side of the frog. But we seem to be in a vicious circle - the less she'll let us get at that foot, the worse it gets; the more we try to treat it, the more violent her kicking gets. It's such a shame because until she had that abscess, I'm sure she didn't mind her feet being done at all. The bill was £17 but I told Mark to keep the £20 note. "It's called bribery and corruption," I told him. Face running in sweat, he didn't demur.

SEPTEMBER 23RD

Q took Chloe riding while I dressed up Bella. Determined not to make the same mistake of tying her to a moveable object like the trailer, but left with nothing immovable around (for I suspect she could pull down the whole block of stables if she took a mind to it,) I decided just to keep hold of the lunge line attached to her halter while I put everything on. She stood like a lamb – maybe she thought she was tied up. I lunged her for a short while with no problems and then walked her up the drive. A lovely, satisfying day. Tonight I wondered about Diane's insistence of making Bella trot on the lunge. Is it actually necessary for a horse who will always be doing everything at the walk?

September 27th

John Wones brought the trolley at long last. It's not the smartest in the world, but it looks perfectly OK for around here. Now to persuade Q to put up a shelter for it and the tumbril. John also kindly enlightened me on the "whipple tree" we've been using – apparently we've been working a spreader bar meant for separating two horses in trace harness! He said we need chains running from the hooks on the hames down to a proper whipple tree and then we hook the harrow or whatever on to that. We learn something new every day. I sometimes think Diane and I are a case of the blind leading the partially sighted...

September 28th

Des and his mates were crashing around in the stables, so we harnessed up Bella round the front of the house and then long-reined her up the drive pulling a tyre. She was jumpy at first at the strange noise behind her but she soon settled and plodded along quite happily. "Where do we go from here?" asked Diane. The answer is, I don't know. Do we keep doing a little but two or three times a week, or rest her all winter? I'm hoping someone on Sunday will tell me.

October 1st

A marvellous day out at the Autumn Working Day, organised by the ECHHA. Chloe came with me and proved a lovely companion, taking a great interest in everything. Lots of horsemen with Shires, Percherons, Suffolks and crosses, carting, rolling, harrowing and ploughing, but not many members of the public. The atmosphere was friendly and informal and I felt happy about asking for advice. I learnt so much: to cover my harrows with hawthorn to convert them to a chain harrow for grass; that there is no need for a back band and crupper but that the plough band helps keep the chains up; that most people tie their plough lines to the bit with any old knot. Gilbert told me that he's got a light plough suitable for Bella which I must follow up. Bob Peacock says to ring him on Wednesday evening for a phone number for proper plough lines. The general consensus of opinion was to keep messing about with her during the winter, rather than turn her away, but not to do so much that she gets bolshi. Watching the youngsters walk around the ring, I wished that I'd had the courage to take Bella. She's so much prettier than any of them there. Maybe one day.

OCTOBER 9TH

Fun and games today. Des and Co were making a noise down at the stables and a cement mixer was due at 10.30 am, so Diane and I decided not to hang about but to get up the drive. Q collected a tractor tyre for me on Saturday but we have no fixings for it so we elected just to long-rein. The cattle were all by the fence which caused great excitement. Bella stopped, wheeled round and then shot off. But we hung on and eventually she calmed down although not really settling. On the way back the bridle broke – typically it was the very first time we'd taken her out without the halter too. So we bodged a halter with the lunge line and hoped she'd be none the wiser. She wasn't.

October 13th

The stable walls are finished; all Q has to do is remove the tiles and the new roof can go on. Then we can clear the ground for the yard and soon it'll be ready for the animals' return. I shall be happier to see them off the river bank. Bella's feet are splitting, Humphrey is still lame where Crispin had to cut away the outer part of his foot and William's feet look none too healthy. I didn't want to feed them this early on in the winter (especially William who still looks pregnant) but I'm giving them all Biotition and food is the only way to get it in them. Bella is on Quiet Mix with Equivite and Bio, while the donks have a small handful of flaked maize and Bio. At £8.60 a tub, I hope it does some good. They've been having wads of hay for just over a week now, but it's only in the past couple of days that they've really been tucking into it. We're getting through ½ to ¾ of a bale a day. Soon it will be time to start feeding properly – the Clarks recommended sugar beet pulp, mangolds, carrots and oats. Stan Hammond used to feed bran as well, but according to current opinion, that's no longer recommended. I don't want Bella hotting up on oats, and I can't find mangolds, so she'll get Quiet Mix, sugar beet pulp, flaked maize, barley and carrots. I have to make sure I don't overfeed to avoid the danger of something called azoturia (I think that's right) which is a kind of cramp due to too much food and not enough work.

October 16th

It must be a couple of weeks since Bella had to work hard at pulling and today she proved that she really is broken to chains, as they say. We put her straight on to pulling the girders in the field, and after a head-high start she stepped round like she's done it all her life. It's impossible to describe the satisfaction of controlling a heavy horse simply by lines and command. She was magnificent, pacing herself steadily as she pulled the girders. She certainly knows her commands – you only have to say 'come here' or 'wheesh' and she turns left or right without touching her mouth at all. She also seems to understand 'no' better than trying to command her to do the things you want instead. She is beginning to grow her winter woollies but she is still glossy and gleaming. Diane says she looks the picture of health.

OCTOBER 18TH

Blue skies, golden leaves glowing in the autumn sunshine – and Diane couldn't come! It was too good a morning to waste, so rather than risk making a fool of myself with Bella in front of the builders, I took William for a drive to the yellow gates. Poor old chap – he's so unfit and as unwilling as ever! He has a heart of gold: if only he enjoyed going out. It's probably having to pull the cart up the ghastly drive; the road would obviously be more enjoyable for him. Diane came after tea but we couldn't do much as Bella got doubly spooked catching her hip on the gate and by the noise of the builders. She's so used to peace and quiet that people standing on the roof and throwing things around totally unnerves her. She worked herself into a proper sweat even though we only long-reined her round the field.

OCTOBER 28TH

The stables and yard are finished so Bella and the donks moved back – and not a day too soon with autumn gales and sweeping rain. Bella went bananas when she saw the yard and I only just managed to get her halter off before she shot off, farting and snorting with excitement. William too was het up, while I completely lost hold of Humphrey. He set off up the drive while Bella and William galloped alongside, the right side of the fence. They all settled down eventually although William and Humphrey seemed very peeved at being shut up. Tonight Bella is standing guard outside her friends' door.

OCTOBER 30TH

Two steps forward, ten back. Lucky I wasn't demonstrating how I've broken Bella to chains today! Not only has she had over a week's lay-off, but there was also a strong wind blowing, making it difficult for her to hear me. She seemed to have totally lost confidence, backing up, rearing, trotting, swinging round. My priority today was just keeping out of Bella's way!

NOVEMBER 1ST

Well, it wasn't the wind this morning but Bella was still awful. We gave up trying to pull and just long-reined her round the field. Whatever can it be? Is she bored? Is it too long or too short a break?

NOVEMBER 3RD

We called Bella as usual this morning but instead of trotting up eagerly, she kicked up her heels and galloped off. She then spent the next 10 minutes having the most terrific game with the donkeys, chasing them round and round the field. Eventually she skidded to a halt, nostrils flared and blowing, flanks heaving. We decided it would be best to take her straight out of the field rather than try and work her in her playground. We started off as usual, Diane on the lines and me at her head, but to my horror she started to crush me against the fence and then rear, despite Diane's desperate efforts to pull her off me. For a few seconds I had a dreadful vision of those gigantic hooves trampling me into the ground. A timely reminder of how dangerous a young heavy horse can be; Roger Clark's "lethal machines" echoed through my brain. So we unhitched the tyre and long-reined her, pulling just the whipple tree, to the pump house and back. Then we attached the tyre and went to the bridge and back. By now she was tired and sweaty and reasonably resigned. So we won in the end, but with what an effort. I suppose we must accept these setbacks and not be disheartened.

NOVEMBER 10TH

We should have been working Bella today; instead Diane and I collected Martini, Chloe's first pony. We saw her last week-end and Chloe loved her. Diane approved of her and Crispin vetted her (only suggesting that a little lemon and soda might help liven her up!), and so after handing over £700 we took home one 13.2 chestnut mare, saddle and bridle. To ensure that she doesn't pass any infection to the other three, we put her on her own on the river bank. She accepted it all quite calmly, grazing contentedly within minutes. Bella, on the other hand, was quite mad with frustration. She caught glimpses of the pony and could hear her but, oh how infuriating, she couldn't get near her. I hope she doesn't trample Martini to death when they do get together. It occurred to me today that if I hadn't met Diane I would probably just be living here quietly with

William and Humphrey. Although I'd always dreamed of owning a Shire, it would have remained just that, a dream, if it hadn't been for Diane. And now here I am with a second horse and I've always loathed children's ponies! Martini's saving grace, in my eyes, is that she looks like a mini Shire, with her kind eyes, heavy bones and feathered feet.

NOVEMBER 14TH

Mark came this morning. Martini will need new shoes in a month but otherwise she's OK; both donks have a touch of seedy toe and Bella's foot is still a mess but no worse. She tried to give Mark a fractured skull when he went to pick up one of her front feet, but he gave her a good kick back, in the tummy, and she was quite good after that. He remains optimistic that she will behave eventually. I do admire his tenacity! His plans for a forge at his home are nearing completion, and he hopes then to cut down a lot of his travelling. I asked him whether he thought I'd be taking Bella to him – not owning a suitable lorry - and he laughed and said "No, I'll still come out and see people like you."

NOVEMBER 15TH

Diane schooled Martini this morning and then we led her up the drive along with Wilbur. We passed swans, cows and a tractor – none of which bothered Martini in the slightest. She really does seem to be placid. Then it was Bella's turn. Since we'd already walked nearly two miles, we decided to walk Bella just along the river bank, a new experience for her. She was lovely, walking quickly but quietly. We must get her pulling again. I can't think why I worried about Bella hurting Martini. That little old pony is definitely the Queen Bee. Bella seems quite devoted to her already, even though she is definitely kept in her place, with the odd kick and bite.

NOVEMBER 22ND

A disastrous day. We long-reined Bella up the drive and she went happily and steadily. So we put on the tyre, and while I was hooking on the chains, Diane said, "How quietly she's standing – she's obviously in a nice mood." Scarcely were the words out of her mouth than Bella took off. Diane couldn't hold on, so Bella careered off down the drive, complete with whipple tree and bouncing tyre. She finally came to a panting halt at the bridge and, having caught up, we were just managing to disentangle everything when she wheeled round, knocking Diane and I flying and set off for home. As she rounded the last corner by the house the tyre hit the fence and smashed the whipple tree in half, and then she dashed headlong through the barbed wire back to the stables. She was blowing hard by the time Diane and I limped our way up to her so we unhitched the chains and then long-reined her up the drive. She obviously needed to pull again, but she seemed paranoid at the noise of the chains so we decided to call it a day.

This evening I realised how hard the chains must have caught me as she wheeled round: my legs are covered in ugly scarlet weals. "Has it put you off?" Diane asked me as we recovered over coffee. Maybe she was hoping it had, but surprisingly it hasn't. I know today's experience has set us back, but we will win, I feel sure of it. My resolve was further strengthened when coincidentally Stan Hammond rang to see how she was. As I told him about the latest fiasco, I grew even more determined that I will not be beaten. Killed maybe, but not beaten! "That horse has got a good home," declared Stan. "I hope she knows it." I hope so too.

A barn owl has found a good home too - unfortunately, perched on the rafter above my car so every morning there's a mess on the windscreen that looks exactly like a pot of paint has been emptied over it. It's lovely to have him (her?) though; he's so sure of us now that we can drive right underneath his perch and his huge unblinking eyes balefully regard us as we get out of the car. I do hope he's getting rid of some of our mice although I fear our rats are too massive for him to tackle. I found one yesterday that was as big as a rabbit.

NOVEMBER 23RD

Two bruised and battered women went to work on one wilful horse. We simply lunged and long-reined today in an attempt to regain Bella's confidence. At first she was twitchy with a stress line clearly showing down her side, but she eventually settled although she was reluctant to for any length of time. We must concentrate on getting her to stand quite still for longer periods. To make up for lost ground, Diane is coming tomorrow, and again on Saturday. We shall overcome!

NOVEMBER 27TH

Gloom, despair, depression. We attached the chains and whipple tree and before she'd even tried to walk normally, she bolted back to her stable, crashing into the fence on the way. We took her out of the stable, disentangled everything and then put on the saddle and full breeching. To our amazement she took it quite calmly and then we long-reined her round the yard. It is tempting to give up sometimes.

November 29th

Bella is once again getting increasingly difficult to catch. One look at the two of us, and she's off – heels high. Then she comes past us at full gallop, spraying us with mud, almost as if to giggle, "You can't catch me, hee hee." Finally she stands well away, daring us to approach. We resist the temptation to let her make fools of us and shake a bucket of nuts instead. Then, stomach wins the day and, warily, she agrees to come up.

We long-reined Bella round the yard again, fully harnessed and she went well. Perhaps because she feels close to home. Diane suggested we attach the chains and walk behind, but I said I was sure that she wasn't frightened of either the chains or pulling, but of me behind her. Diane thought we were asking for trouble but agreed, reluctantly, to give it a go. So I attached the chains, leaving them trailing and then went and sat on a bale in full view of Bella. To our amazement, the idea worked. Bella was brilliant.

December 2nd

This time we long-reined with chains trailing and then attached them to the whipple tree. No problems. Perhaps we are making progress again at last.

December 4th

Again, chains and whipple tree but moving slightly off the

yard, taking her further from home. She panicked when her hoof slipped on the icy ground, but she seems to be gaining confidence. You can see her listening to our words of reassurance.

December 13th

We are getting nowhere. Bella stands calmly and contentedly while we put the harness on and attach the chains and whipple tree. And then, for no reason at all, she takes off. Diane let go on Monday and again today. I can't blame her. I defy anyone to hold a ton of bolting horse. But what's so frustrating is that she doesn't bolt because she's frightened but because she's bloody minded and knows we can't hold her. I feel unutterably depressed after today's session. We have to do something, but I don't know what.

December 15th

Mark came to shoe Martini and trim the others. Bella stunned us both by behaving impeccably. She lifted each foot in turn and held it quite patiently as though to the manner born. Mark was pleased with her improved performance but disheartened at the continuing problem of her back foot. Humphrey made up for Bella by bucking, rearing and kicking, but at least he's a rather more manageable size.

December 18th

Black Monday indeed. I rang Cheryl Clark to ask her advice. It was brief and to the point. "Shoot her. If that horse has taken off that many times you'll never be able to trust her.

Some horses just take off and she's obviously one of them." I asked Cheryl about hobbling, knowing it's a practice she believes in, but "If you don't know what you're doing you can break her neck." She said what Bella needed was a helluva fright but when asked how, she said those were "the tricks of the trade." I suspect they involve bringing a horse to its knees which I wouldn't be able to do, so knowing Cheryl's tricks wouldn't help anyway. Cheryl is due for an operation on her leg this Friday and will be out of action for at least a month. "Ring me at the end of January and I'll see what I can do but I can't guarantee anything. As I say, the best thing to do with a horse like her is shoot it." And just to add to my woes, Chloe is having problems with Martini who is proving considerably more high-spirited and uncontrollable than we thought. So much for Crispin's ice and lemon! I should have stuck to donkeys.

DECEMBER 22ND

The general feeling is that Bella will never be trustworthy as a working horse. She may be fine for six months, a year even, but then she could take off and that would be lethal. I am heartbroken. After all this time and effort – to say nothing of expense – it seems I have no choice but to sell her.

JANUARY 4TH

David Banham came to see Bella. He offered me £800 for her, the harness and the tumbril. Said he wasn't really interested as he'd got four working geldings, but that she was a nice looking horse. Bella was distinctly unimpressed by him, sidling up to his attractive wife instead. Two hours later he returned with Jack Juby, suddenly full of ideas of breeding. Upped the price to £1,000. Jack liked Bella but said she was too duck-arsed, not Roman-nosed enough and too long-legged for show quality.

January 9th

I rang David Banham and agreed the deal. Eight hundred pounds for Bella, £100 for the harness and £100 for the tumbril. He said Jack Juby would like to buy Martini but Chloe says no. Jack Juby is super: like so many heavy horsemen, small, wiry and quiet with a good head of white hair despite his 72 years. He has trained horses, broken, worked, jumped and shown horses: Suffolks, Shires, Percherons and Hackneys. He broke his first horse when he was 10, and has worked with them since he left school at 14. He believes his extraordinary skill in handling horses - a skill well-known throughout the country - is like a disease and that you're either afflicted with it or you're not. I wish it was Jack Juby rather than the burly David Banham buying Bella.

January 12th

I have cried myself to sleep for two nights now. Will Banham love her as much as I do? Will she be happy yarded instead of running free? What if he tires of breeding or Bella fails to produce a foal? I like David Banham, and I've not heard much said against him – at least, no more than the usual backbiting. But his enthusiasm seems to be so sudden and his ideas so grandiose. He's only been into Shires for a few years, after all. Bella is just two – where will David Banham be in 20 years' time?

This morning I put Bella's harness on for some last photographs. She looked so beautiful, gleaming in the sunshine, peacefully dozing behind her blinkers. I cried my eyes out all over her nose. After I'd finished, John Wones rang to say everyone knew about "bolting Bella" and that I was selling her and did I want another filly he'd heard about? I told him, no, I was certainly not going to start all over again. This was the end of my Shire experiences. He asked how much I was selling her for and said that was far too little, bearing in mind her breeding, and even knowing her problem. And then suddenly I decided. It isn't the money – I just cannot, will not let Bella go. I rang Banham straight away and although I should have felt guilty at reneging on the deal, I felt over the moon. I know I've made the right decision.

JANUARY 15TH

Talk about telepathy! Just as I'm looking up Stan Hammond's number, he rings me! He wanted to know how I was getting on and so I told him the whole sorry tale (thank God I didn't have to admit that I'd given up, all for a measly £800) and he wasn't nearly as pessimistic as the rest. He reckons that because she's still a baby we can beat it by using a Liverpool bit and curb chain and, if necessary, pulling her on to her backside. "You do that a few times and she'll soon learn," he said brightly. He agreed that it would be a good idea to breed from her – to cover my odds, so to speak – and suggested Bryan Banham's stallion, Hilmore Mascot (Bryan is no relation of David). "Don't hurt yourself," warned Stan, "I'd never forgive myself if you got hurt." Bless him – he's as lovely as the filly he bred.

January 25th

Bella's stable is open to the sky! I came home from work to find asbestos all over the place, even as far as Q's boat. How it missed all the animals, I'll never know. They must have been terrified as it all took off. Builders from Surlingham have promised to fix it as soon as these gales subside.

The river was magic tonight. The wind running against the tide whipped up huge waves, sending the geese and ducks scuttling to the banks for safety. We're on flood alert – yet again – but I'm not worried. If this house didn't get wet in the great floods of '53, I don't think it ever will. Anyway, there's nothing I can do to stop it coming over, so my philosophy is just to go to bed and forget about it. If the house is under water in the morning too bad. . . There's no point choosing to live just a few feet from a river and then worrying about flooding.

February 27th

A long break from this diary, but Bella has not been neglected. She's got very good at standing patiently while I groom her from top to toe. I pick up all her feet except the "funny" one. As I brush that leg she always raises her foot and I'm not sure whether she's trying to be helpful or warning me. So far, I haven't dared to find out! Today I visited Bryan Banham to view Mascot. In fact, Bryan never materialised, but his groom, Greg, showed me around. Hilmore Mascot is superb – 18.1hh and with such a long, shaggy forelock that he looks just like an old English sheepdog. But most importantly, he's got a lovely temperament – which is why Stan suggested him – and the kindest eyes ever, when you lift up the hair. He's definitely the chap for Bella come May. Greg too is lovely; helpful and interested and clearly Mascot thinks so too. Apparently when he needs to prepare the stallion for showing he sits on his back to shampoo his mane!

MARCH 1ST

The Liverpool bit has arrived. It looks very big and shiny and, at £43, let's hope it does the trick.

MARCH 6TH

The big day at last. If Diane and I can't hold Bella in a Liverpool we must accept defeat. The wind was blowing across the marshes which was not ideal, but at least it was dry, making it easier for us all to keep our feet. We dressed Bella for the first time since December 18th. The 6 inch Liverpool fits perfectly and Bella didn't seem to mind. Then we long-reined her out to the tractor tyre. I hooked the chains on to the hames while Diane stood at Bella's head. I think we were both feeling somewhat apprehensive – it wasn't only our pride at risk of being hurt. Then I took the lunge line on the right and Diane stepped back to the left with the plough lines. Bella made to plunge forward but the bit and the weight of the tyre pulled her up short. We urged her on and she tried to turn, to back and to plunge and then... one chain came unhooked from the whipple tree. We unhooked, re-tied and tried again. After a few more stops and starts, she set off and we actually managed to circle the field. It was such a fantastic thrill. Unfortunately she suddenly decided to step back on the last stretch and put her foot over the chain. We decided to call it a day and she stood quite quietly while we pulled the chain back across one foot. She really is extraordinarily good at being messed about – there are obviously advantages to being clumsy! She was hot and sweaty when we got her back (the tractor tyre is no mean weight) but she got lots of hugs and Quiet Mix. Diane and I were very chuffed with ourselves – we'll show all those doubting Banhams and Clarks. (Although we must be cautious – after all, we did have her pulling well once before when she suddenly decided to take off. But I feel optimistic).

MARCH 7TH

From bolter to immovable. To start with, Bella refused to move at all and so, very reluctantly, as it was obviously a highly vulnerable position, I moved forward so that she could see me and gain confidence. She then moved forward and eventually lowered her head and plodded round remarkably steadily. Diane and I are both feeling confident again and starting to plan our course of action once more. The vital thing, I believe, is not to bore her by endlessly pulling that tyre round the field and yet she needs a lot more practice at stopping and starting smoothly. I will try backing her when Diane can't come and some time soon we shall balance some poles along her flanks to give her the idea of shafts.

MARCH 13TH

Not a success. After jibbing and backing, Bella finally agreed to move forward – only to break the whipple tree! But in the meantime I've been doing lots of backing with Bella and she no longer looks so puzzled at being asked to reverse.

March 15th

Diane's husband David has made us a metal whipple tree and we have rounded up some lorry tyres from John Wones (the place is beginning to look like a tyre dump!) We started today with a lorry tyre which is just light enough for us to drag and yet much heavier than a car tyre. But Bella refused to go forward. So we used the whip but still she kept backing and tangling her feet in the chains. I lost count of how many times we unhooked, disentangled and hooked up again. At one time, Bella was actually facing the whipple tree and tyre! Eventually we tried just the whipple tree and she moved forward all right but she was then in danger of being walloped on the back legs by an iron bar which would not have done wonders for her confidence. So we attached the little light car tyre and, wonders will never cease, off went Bella like a lamb. The heavy tractor tyre has certainly given her the shock she needed, but it's also taught her to jib. Now I think we must go back to the beginning, building up her confidence as we slowly increase the weight of the tyre. At least we managed to hang on to her today and nothing broke. We should be grateful for small mercies.

I spoke to Stan Hammond last night. He told me his father kept a breaking horse – one that did no work on the land but whose sole function was to break in the youngsters. He would be harnessed alongside and apparently soon kicked or bit the newcomer into line. He also told me how they'd had one horse who always lay down as his harness was put on. So they got another horse to drag him round the field until he got up and he never lay down again! How did they break a horse to shafts? Simple – work him all day until he was exhausted and then place him between the shafts with one wheel tied. I suspect Stan thinks Diane and I are being far too soft with Bella – but he's too nice and polite to tell me!

MARCH 19TH

Shire Horse Show Day at Peterborough. A glorious day; so
hot and sunny that it was difficult to believe it was only
March. Apparently people were complaining that no one
was selling ice creams! Diane and I watched the three-year-
old class and realised why Bella will never win any prizes.
Jack Juby is quite right: her tail is set too low, her nose
isn't Roman enough and her feet are pudding plate rather
than meatplate sized. But as she matures, so her lankiness
is disappearing; her body is growing in proportion to her
long legs. But despite all that, there wasn't a horse there
that I'd have changed her for. We met Stan Hammond with
Norman and Bridget and had a long chat. Stan suggested
one sharp crack along her ribs would do her more good
than several cracks of the lunge whip. He told me I should
have a party to celebrate finally breaking her and invite all
the doubters! Talking of which, we also met David Banham.
I would swear he was going to pretend he hadn't seen us
but I marched straight up to him and apologised immediately for letting him down on our deal. Having been forced
to acknowledge me – and a little taken aback by my apolo-
gy I suspect – he asked me how I was getting on and I said
she was working well (little white lie?) and that I was going
to breed from her. Next person we bumped into was Bryan
Banham whose manners certainly did not match his dap-
per appearance. But Greg was very welcoming and friendly
and I feel confident that Bella will be safe in his hands. It
was a glorious day out and all three of us enjoyed a holiday feeling, a break from routine. Chloe insisted on saying
hello to each Shire horse there and loved every minute of
it.

March 21st

I thought we were going to have problems today as Bella tried to swing round, but after a little coaxing she moved off and steadily pulled the car tyre round the field several times. She was sweating profusely by the end, from apprehension rather than effort, I think.

March 28th

We are definitely progressing! Today there was a noticeable improvement even on yesterday. She is moving off better now and although there were several little tantrums – in the form of backing or plunging – on the whole she pulled steadily and evenly. She is learning to walk better now - instead of prancing or hopping – as Diane calls it – and we had two very smooth, dare I say professional, move-offs. One more day of work and then she has a week's holiday while Chloe and I explore Kerry with an Irish horse-drawn gypsy caravan.

April 8th

"Whatever do you want to spend your holiday looking up a horse's backside for?" Put so succinctly, I did wonder about the answer. Mary was a sweet, gently-natured 13.2 pony of indeterminate breeding with a top speed of ½ mph (that is, downhill with a tailwind). In one week we covered all of 30 miles travelling from 9 am to around 6 pm. We soon discovered why we were the only caravan on the road: the nights were perishing. I don't think I've ever been so cold and wet in my life. On the Monday we were stopped halfway up a hill while, with frozen fingers, I struggled to undo the chains.

Sleet and hail were sweeping horizontally. A car pulled up and an American woman asked if we were having a lovely time. My answer caused her to leap back into the car and completely forget to wish me a "nice day." That evening I discovered the joys of brandy with a measure of port (and I've never been a spirit drinker!) – and the holiday improved dramatically from that moment on. It was an extraordinary week – more a survival course than a holiday. We lived from day to day – just Chloe, Mary and me. I grew very fond of Mary; I loved the tenacious way she tackled the hills, putting every ounce of strength into the old, ill-fitting collar. "Don't stop the horse on the hill," they'd told us, but Mary obviously hadn't been listening as she would struggle for ten paces, and then stop for a breather before pressing on for another ten. She did exactly as she pleased regardless of what I said or did, so after a while I sat back and let her get on with it. The only time she speeded up was within the last few feet of our stop for the night. No need to worry about where to go, Mary unerringly stopped at the right pubs. Her harness was a splendid Irish hotchpotch and I regret to say that Cheryl Clark's instructions about the correct order of harnessing up disappeared into the Irish mists. I put on whatever came to hand first, trusting Mary not to let me down – and she never did. One day we took the caravan down to a deserted sandy beach, and we unhitched her and walked her, like a dog, along the sea's edge. At one point, she lay down and rolled in the sand, in utter happiness, and her kind, patient eyes seemed to thank us. Chloe rode her bareback along the beach and I had the feeling that she would willingly have tried anything we asked of her.

APRIL 10TH

A week's break has done Bella good. She pulled surprisingly well and smoothly. Which is more than can be said for

Chloe and me: we are both ill. One week of freezing nights and damp clothes has left us both with bronchitis. But Chloe is confirmed in her ambition to be a gypsy. With her long dark hair and luscious eyes and permanent tendency to look unwashed and unkempt she certainly won't have any problem looking the part! As I say to her, she can do whatever she wants as long as she's happy and fulfilled. I suppose because I've always achieved everything I ever wanted, I have no frustrated ambitions to foist on my daughter – unlike so many parents I know.

APRIL 18TH

A milestone in our breaking! Bella went really well in the field and so we took her up the drive, pulling the tyre. It was the first time out, pulling, since that disastrous day four months ago. We turned at the bridge and congratulated ourselves on an uneventful trip.

APRIL 21ST

If only the doubters could have seen us today! We harnessed up and went straight up the drive. She backed up at first and got into a bit of a muddle with the chains, but after that she went like a dream all the way to the yellow gate. We need to practise stopping and starting and tight turns more, but I really believe we are getting there.

APRIL 27TH

"We've cracked it!" declared Diane as the three of us ambled peacefully up the drive. In fact it was four of us as Wilbur came too. Now and then he gave Bella a slight start by suddenly appearing under her blinkers but it won't do her any harm. But now it's me who's sounding the cautious note while Diane is filled with optimism. Certainly I would have loved Cheryl Clark to have seen us today. Bolting horse? Wherever did you get that idea? But I know Cheryl is right: she can surprise us again, without warning.

MAY 1ST

Bella worked today for the very first time - harrowing! We tried two harrows together so there was no danger of her stepping back on to the spikes and at first she jibbed at the extra work. Then she put in a few bucks and rears but in just a short time she settled down to the job in hand. A memorable Mayday indeed!

MAY 15TH

We've done more harrowing up and down in sort of wavy lines so today we decided to pull a tyre up the drive for a change. We chose the next size up which has got lots of spokes in the middle – and just to remind us of the dangers of self-satisfaction Bella reared and tried to wheel round. She stepped back, forgot where the bank was and promptly sat down. I don't know who was the most surprised – her or us! Eventually she settled down and pulled steadily, despite the most awful noise from the hub and spokes. It was so loud that Diane and I could hardly hear ourselves shout. On the way back, Bella had obviously had enough, and for the first time showed flashes of real temper. She stopped, put her ears back and chomped her bottom lip in fury. But we won in the end.

Dragging a tyre up the track helps Bella get accustomed to both pulling and the noise behind her

MAY 16TH

Greg came this evening to take Bella to stud. "I've got a big black man for you at home," he whispered to Bella. But it wasn't tempting enough to induce her into the lorry. So Greg patiently moved each foot in turn up the ramp. I know Bella will be in good hands, but I can't help wishing I hadn't sent her. After all, this breeding idea only arose because we didn't seem to be able to work her. But now, thanks to Stan, I seem to have a working Shire and I don't really want or need (or more importantly can afford to have) a foal. Bryan Banham wants to keep her 28 days after covering to ensure she's in foal, but I don't think I can bear her to be gone that long. Bryan made it plain that I was not welcome to go and see her when I want, but I shall ignore him and fix with Greg to see her next week.

MAY 18TH

It seems so odd without Bella. Martini misses her too, standing by the gate for hours on end and gazing wistfully up the drive. Humphrey and William seem quite unconcerned.

MAY 19TH

I should not go to auctions! I got completely carried away today and spent too much on a beautiful set of trace harness. So much that I daren't even admit it to Diane. It was the ECHHA auction near March which led me astray. I also bought an old whipple tree for £1, a pair of hames for £6 and a back chain for £6. I bought the trace harness because I don't feel a plain plough band is secure enough for such a young, inexperienced horse. I am hoping that the crupper and the hip strap will help to keep everything in place if Bella decides to be funny. No doubt everybody at the auction thought I didn't know what I was buying! One man who wanted the back chain asked me very rudely whether I knew what it was and if I'd actually got a horse. "Yes, thank you" I said sweetly.

It was a very different auction from last year's. Not only were the prices much higher, but a lot of people who I don't know seemed to know who I was. I suppose a blonde in a filthy long Barbour with a child in tow does stand out at an auction like that – they'll certainly know me now after spending so much! I went back to Stan Hammond's for tea along with Bridget and Norman and saw their two foals and Bella's mother. The foals were gorgeous but they did make me wonder yet again whether I'm doing the right thing with Bella. They're so very big and unmanageable at only eight weeks – and what of the cost and potential difficulties? I asked Stan about making Bella back, which I'm not doing very successfully, and he suggested we pull her back on the reins under her mouth and heave on her shoulder at the same time. He seemed genuinely pleased that we're winning – although very disapproving of her long tail! In true Fenland fashion, Stan believes Shire horses should be docked and hairy chins trimmed. I beg to disagree! He told me how Bella's mother had had a nasty habit of backing towards you and then stopping at just the right distance to give you a vicious kick. He'd stopped it by letting her back on to a pitchfork he was holding. "She never did it again," he said, triumphantly. Funny how they never told me about that before I bought Bella! The traditional breeding ground for Shires spreads from Wales in the west to the east coast up to a line from Kendal to Whitby. But the fens have produced the most famous Shires. It's incredible to think that my longing for a Shire of my own dates back to my days as a journalist on a Fen newspaper when I interviewed Graham Ward about the Gorefield Gala. As I drove up to his spacious farmhouse I was struck by the sight of his Shire foals playing in the fields. Graham and his sons have since won several trophies with their superb Shires, stud prefix Decoy.

MAY 22ND

This is what it must be like to have a child at boarding school. All day, I was so excited at the thought of seeing Bella – and then so disappointed that she obviously isn't missing me one jot! She has become great friends with one of Mike Flood's mares and was much more interested in sticking close to her than coming to see me. She seemed a little nervy as she always is when I've been away for a bit, but she looked well and happy enough. Hillmore Mascot just wanders peacefully around all the mares, even those with foals. I've decided to let Bella be covered and then bring her home and cut my losses. (£100 stud fee, £2 per day keep).

MAY 23RD

Just as well Bella is away as Diane has cracked two ribs. Poor girl: some cow backed into her, knocked her over and stood on her. She's in agony at the moment and will probably be out of action for some time. I always told her cattle were dangerous – helping to break a young Shire is obviously the safer bet!

MAY 29TH

Greg rang tonight to say Bella has been covered. She was

covered intentionally on Saturday and possibly on the Friday night as well. He says there were no problems at all, no need for an injection. and she apparently was as good as gold. "In fact she's running him ragged," he laughed. "I had to take Mascot out to give him a break! She's so keen that I thought she was going to jump the dyke to get to him!" Greg is off to the Suffolk Show tomorrow, but he says if she's still in season he'll cover again in the morning and that I can see her on Friday. Roll on Friday!

JUNE 1ST

Chloe and I went to see Bella who deigned to give a snicker of welcome this time, but refused to budge from Mascot's side. It was lovely to see stallion and mare standing so quietly, side by side. The lack of grooming and grass are beginning to show – she certainly lacks the lustre she had when she went. Greg reckons I should take her home. "If she's not in foal it's certainly not for want of trying on her part," he said. So he will bring her home on Monday. I can't wait.

JUNE 5TH

Bella is home! When I saw Greg come through the yellow gate I was over the moon with excitement. Bella was very sweaty and a little snorty and puzzled, but Martini bellowed a greeting, galloped up to her – and then squealed and kicked her. Some homecoming! But I suppose Martini just needed to remind her big friend that although she might have been away, she was still the boss. Within a short time they settled down, grazing quietly nose to nose. I knew I'd missed Bella but tonight I realised just how much. I wish I didn't have to go to work tomorrow, but on

Thursday I shall wash, brush and fuss her to my heart's content.

JUNE 6TH

Oh, the magic of having Bella safely home again! This afternoon, Bella was lying down dozing. So I went and stroked her while her great head sank down into the mud, her nose and mouth squashed and her eyes closed. Then with a look over her shoulder at me, she stretched out full while I squatted next to her and stroked her neck. Incredible to think that just six months ago she would always get up when approached – yet now her trust in me is such that she lies vulnerable and exposed, fast asleep with me next to her. William broke the spell by rolling over and catching her with his hooves!

JUNE 7TH

I took Bella round to the stables for a wash and brush up. I brushed and brushed her until I started to sweat and she started to gleam. Then I picked out her front feet, she tried to pull away but I hung on. How the hell does she manage to stand on two feet, I've got one and she tries to get me with a back foot? Then I decided to look at the tricky back one because she's certainly keeping her weight off it. I wrapped the sheet round and then pulled it up on to a bale of hay. She stood quite quietly while I poked and pumped a bottle of hydrogen peroxide in. The hoof seems to have decayed away and the frog looks very large, spongy and moveable. I'm glad it's only another week before Mark comes. Then I washed her legs and feathers with Lux and again she stood without complaint, even while I did the back ones. She looked so lovely afterwards with four really white legs – even if it does only last a short time. I then tried on the new trace harness but decided that without a helping hand on the other side, I couldn't manage it. It really is incredibly heavy, much more so than the saddle and breeching. We'd done so well that I didn't want to spoil things. One the way back to the river bank she accidentally brushed my toe with her foot. Thank heavens for steel-capped boots. Greg is quite right: Bella has no idea where her feet are! He said he'd never known such a clumsy-footed horse.

JUNE 12TH

Having long-reined Bella brilliantly up the drive on Friday, I felt perfectly confident about setting off again today. Silly me. Bella played up by continually stopping or turning round. I gave up in the end but rather than let her get off scot free I practised reversing on the yard. For one ghastly moment at first I thought she was going to rear on me but I yanked her head down and then she backed superbly... with the help of a few peppermints.

JUNE 14TH

Diane back today, although still a little sore. We put the new trace harness on which looks great, although the belly band seems to be in the wrong place and the bar bangs behind her legs. After a bit of a fuss, she pulled the smallest tyre up the drive. She really is very good the way she takes all our inexpert fumbling and messing about with remarkable equanimity.

June 15th

Mark came and showed great concern over Bella's back foot. The frog had grown enormously which it will, he said, if there's no ground to stop it, but he admitted to not understanding why it was becoming detached. He couldn't find any maggots and yet something seems to be eating it away. He cut out a piece of frog bigger than a man's fist and took it away with him. The bar in her foot seems to have disappeared, again he's at a loss to understand why. He's trimmed away her toe as much as possible to force her to stand on the heel and I noticed that immediately she is putting her weight on that foot so he has obviously relieved a little of the discomfort. He doesn't know what to suggest.

June 19th

Looking at pictures I have discovered that there is no need for the bar on the harness since Bella is not in front of another horse. So I have removed it. Poor Bella – what we do to her in ignorance! In fact what we had left banging on her back legs was a spreader bar, like the one we used as a whipple tree until John Wones put us right. She makes no fuss about the crupper, no doubt she thinks it's yet another one of our many mistakes!

June 28th

I have a plough! I was telling Jimmy Loades about trying to get a plough off Gilbert when he suddenly announced that he's got a pony plough. He says he's happy for me to borrow it for as long as I want but that he doesn't want to sell it. Suits me. Jimmy admired my new Mercedes and I explained that I couldn't really afford such an extravagant car and to prepare for seeing me on a bike when poverty overtook me. But he said: "I'll only believe you're hard up when you sell that horse of yours!"

July 2nd

Today we experimented with imitation shafts, using two trellis poles from the garden centre. By mistake Diane poked Bella up the nose with the end of one which wasn't the best of starts, and then we tried them in the wrong place so that they poked her in the cheek! Eventually we got it right, I think, having sorely tried Bella's patience, and we long-reined her up the drive with the poles in place. At one moment, she decided she was fed up and started backing – not a pretty sight seeing two sharp points coming your way – but with a few cross words she agreed to press on. She came back very placidly, despite the "shafts" swinging alarmingly as they worked their way loose.

July 8th

I laid out two thick planks of wood about 3 feet apart, put on Bella's bridle and practised backing her. I backed her all round the yard, rewarding her regularly with titbits, until she lost the wary look in her eye. Then I backed her between the planks. She jumped a bit when one hoof touched a plank, but she soon relaxed and went in and out with no problems. The lesson is for me as much as her: learning to press lightly on her left shoulder and pull gently on the bridle to the left to move her backside to the right. (At least backing a horse is easier than a trailer; a skill which still eludes me). I shall practise more, reducing the width between the shafts and then raising them on bales. It's so frustrating: here I am with a horse ready to try in shafts and no suitable cart to put her to. Neither Gilbert nor John have anything they can lend and John is too busy to make anything up. So I have no choice but to order a £800 job from Charlie Pinney. It will take up to six weeks which is a pain but it will be ideal when it comes, I hope.

JULY 11TH

Did Bella have to work tonight! We hitched her up to Gilbert's sledge and loaded on about eight bales. With the first load, she flatly refused to pull it up the last little bit to the yard and stood there making ghastly noises in her throat. Was the crupper band too tight and therefore pulling the collar too high on her windpipe? We really didn't know but we slackened it off anyway and she seemed better, although she still wouldn't lower her head and neck into the collar. By the fourth load we decided she had probably had enough so we wisped her down and put her in the stable with a bucket of Quiet Mix while we trailered some more loads in. It was so satisfying to see Bella bringing in the hay while the sun set magnificently over the marshes. Gilbert's sledge is marvellous and it was good of him to lend it to me. It would have been very easy for Q to make one for me but he doesn't seem to have the time.

JULY 22ND

Yesterday I did a round trip of nearly 800 miles to collect my breaking cart from Charlie Pinney – six-and-a-half hours there (due to heavy holiday traffic) and six-and-a-half hours back (due to a heavy load behind me). Charlie rang yesterday to say the cart was ready and since he'd done it so quickly it seemed churlish not to go and get it straight away. So I organised Q to look after Chloe (she'd have been bored with such a very long car journey), hired a 5 x 4 trailer which Charlie assured me would be big enough, and set off with Wilbur for company and protection in the event of a breakdown. Charlie is splendid – tall, good-looking in a rugged kind of way and very forthright with the sort of language that turns the air a deep shade of indigo. We spent a long time loading the cart; I say we but in fact I mostly stood around while he loaded it as he obviously had the strength and know-how. He gave me lots of good tips like having all the chains and belly band relatively tight as it is the movement of the shafts and vibration of the cart that is most frightening at first. He didn't agree with Stan Hammond's idea of tying a wheel but did suggest we start in an enclosed area like a yard so she can't go anywhere else. He says to take it very slowly - back her in first and just jiggle the shafts next to her and then let her out if she seems at all bothered. When she is harnessed in, then just one step at a time to begin with. But when we do go out he suggests that it is safer to get in the cart with the reins, with one person on a safety line rather than try and drive from outside the cart. Diane will be thrilled at the prospect I'm sure. I arrived home well after midnight and so left the cart where it was and unloaded and erected it this morning. I think it looks like £821 well spent: £172 for the basic chassis, £110 for the shafts and brackets, £195 for the wheels and axle and £124 for the bench seat and £220 for the tip cart complete with detachable sides. I think we shall have lots of fun with it and it might even prove an investment. Charlie told me of one chap who sold his for £20 more than he'd paid Charlie for it, much to Charlie's disgust! While I was there, Charlie showed me his Ardennes. Two of them were the most massive horses I've ever seen – legs literally like elephants'. They made Bella seem like a thoroughbred! Charlie runs heavy horse courses and he told me how one of the girls who had never been out of London nearly took off when she saw the size of his horses. Having seen them at unnervingly close quarters, I can sympathise. Working with something that size would terrify me, but perhaps it's just a case of knowing your own animal. Confidence and trust have to be mutual.

July 23rd

To take some of the steam out, we got Bella pulling the sledge around the field. Not very successfully. She didn't seem to settle at all and I think it's because something is pulling the collar back so that it's too tight on her throat. We had the strap in the very last hole and the crupper was several inches below her tail but instead of the collar pulling it up it seems to pull the collar back. We shall have to get someone like Gilbert or Bob Bussingham down to put us straight. We then changed the harness and backed Bella into the cart. While Diane held her head, I hitched up. It took us quite a while to get it right, but Bella didn't seem to mind - she simply dozed in the sunshine. I suppose she is used to us fumbling about. I don't have a belly band – or wanty as Cheryl would say – so I used the lead line. The back chain I bought at the sale is fine but I don't know how to fasten it. I remember Charlie talking about D rings but for the life of me, I can't remember what he said. I shall have to ring him and find out. Otherwise all seemed fine. We took just a couple of reluctant steps forward - she'd far rather have stood there dozing – and rattled and banged the cart about a bit before releasing her. Not bad for a start.

July 29th

We pulled the tyre up the drive and then harnessed Bella into the cart. (I've learnt from Charlie that the D shackle he was talking about is for attaching the back chain to the shafts). We harnessed her tightly, as he recommended, and then took a few steps round the yard. She seemed quite unconcerned about the whole thing.

July 30th

We moved the cart out into the field, then harnessed Bella in. The tug chains are pigs to do up and even worse to undo. I know physique isn't really a requirement when working a heavy horse – but sometimes a man's muscles would come in very handy! We took several steps today with Bella following Diane's hand at her head and me on the lunge line. Again, there were no signs of apprehension or concern at all. In fact, after we'd unhitched her, she stood quietly between the shafts for ages while we talked. Monday is going to be the big day – with Diane driving from the cart I hope. I wish we had somewhere smaller and flatter to start with, than a four acre, very rough field.

July 31st

Diane arrived without her hard hat. David has apparently told her she should long-rein from outside the cart because he doesn't want her to get hurt. With the best will in the world, David does not know about breaking horses; Charlie Pinney certainly does and I respect his opinion that we are safer in the cart than out. My point was nearly tragically proved. Bella reared up at one point, Diane staggered back but not fast enough and would have been trampled on if I hadn't hung on to my lunge line and pulled her off. I offered to ride in the cart but Diane agrees that she is best on the reins, being far more experienced at driving. There is no doubt about this - even Bella knows the difference between us! Of course working with Bella is potentially dangerous – but I feel it is more dangerous to be trampled on than to fall out of the cart. Diane does not agree.

August 1st

We long-reined Bella backwards and forwards across the field in a reasonable attempt at straight lines. Then we backed her between the shafts. She is getting an absolute ace at side-stepping them completely. The advantage of this cart, as opposed to something like a tumbril, is that we can cheat by manoeuvring the cart so that Bella ends up in the right place. She played up a bit at first, then pulled the cart fairly happily round the field with Diane on the reins - well back, at my insistence – and me on the lunge line. If she's good tomorrow one of us really must get into that cart.

August 2nd

Diane in the cart for the first time and Bella seemed much happier. Diane's fears about Bella being unnerved by a different angle on the reins proved groundless. In fact Bella noticeably relaxed, probably because Diane's weight stopped the cart bouncing about so much, making it easier to pull.

I sold the sheep today. After the flock tripled, practically overnight, I decided I simply couldn't cope with the work that they demand. So to Q's disgust, I advertised them as needing good homes and they've all gone - except Lucky (how can you sell something you've bottlefed and thinks it's a dog?) and Rosie (to keep him company). I had a few problems getting rid of Rambo as nobody wanted a ram, but I finally persuaded the Bygone Museum at Fleggburgh to take him, along with two ewes.

AUGUST 17TH

Bella has had a long break while we have been in Yorkshire, so she was somewhat on her toes. We long-reined her round the field and she just didn't want to stand still at all. As for backing between the shafts, well... it's amazing how accurately Bella can step out of the shafts. I swear if I was blinkered I wouldn't be half so good at knowing where those shafts were. But despite her awkwardness and our having to cheat by pulling the cart up to her, she went remarkably well and Diane jumped in for a few minutes. Again, she was much better with the driver in the driving seat - Charlie Pinney knows his stuff! We are not making life easy for her though with such a rough field. Diane says you only realise how rutted it is when you sit in the cart! The heatwave continues and the ground is hard as iron with great cavities opening up. Poor Bella's nose needs regular creamings of zinc and castor oil to stop it blistering in the sun. But at least the dry weather must be helping her foot.

AUGUST 26TH

I fancied doing some harrowing so I persuaded Q to hook up the chains while I held the reins. (Will I ever be able to manage this alone?) It took ages to get Bella to move off, despite hisses, claps and yells, and I had nightmarish visions of her belting off in a hurry when she did finally decide to go. So Q got the whip and with one light crack she moved off smoothly and then harrowed up and down as calmly as anything. Q said nothing but I think he was both surprised and impressed. I keep reading in Heavy Horse World about what a great job wives do, working quietly and essentially behind the scenes while the husbands take all the glory. How I wish I had a wife!

AUGUST 29TH

My first ride in the cart! It was enormously exciting although a little unnerving until I got used to how much more pull on the reins there is compared to long-reining or harrowing. I shall have to do something about padding the seat, though, every turn and bump caught me on the backside and the spine, so that I felt horribly bruised by the time I got out. But very thrilled as well.

SEPTEMBER 2ND

Chloe and I went to the Claxton Show which was great fun. It was all very informal and friendly, exactly like an old-fashioned country show should be. As well as several heavy horses harrowing, ploughing, rolling and giving the children rides, there were lots of children and their ponies competing very uncompetitively. Next year we shall have to take Martini! I chatted to Gilbert and a couple called Barnes who were ploughing with a 20-year-old Shire - their second-ever attempt at it. Everyone was very helpful and encouraging except Paul Heiney who was his usual abrupt self. Still, at least I got the information from him that I wanted: he had three answers to his ad for a hay turner ranging in price from £50 to £175, which gives me some

Bella takes Diane and Chloe for a ride: the hard hats indicate our lack of confidence!

sort of guide line. Good old Bob Bussingham promised to come and give me a ploughing lesson when the ground's a bit softer, perhaps in a week. He asked me if I'd got over the bolting problem - "what you want is a bit of weight on you, girl" he chuckled as he looked me up and down. Looking at his jolly, roly-poly figure I knew what he meant. Bob moves slowly but surely, but his knowledge of ploughing is apparently unrivalled. According to Roger Clark, he is one of the few left who can single line plough.

SEPTEMBER 3RD

Bella went like a dream in the cart this morning. She seems so much happier once one of us is in the cart to weight it down that we've decided next time I get straight in rather than frighten her to start with by letting it bounce over the ruts. I felt extraordinarily happy – it is exhilarating to be driving her at last. She's even learning to lower her head and lean properly into the collar. It will be so valuable to have Bob down to tell me why the collar slips up and back with the trace harness. After lunch Mark came. He reckons her foot is no worse, no better and he's worried that we're running out of time to keep it dry with winter looming now. I gave him the close-up photographs Chloe took of the foot and he promised to get a second opinion. It's obviously not too painful at the moment as she let Mark do all four without a murmur. Afterwards Chloe rode Martini round the fields, way out on her own. Her confidence and ability are improving rapidly, largely thanks to Joan Gunton. We took Martini to Joan, an experienced horse-woman and instructress with no axe to grind, for her opinion on what we should do: buy a smaller pony or battle on. After taking endless trouble Joan's verdict was that we'd got a lovely pony and that we should hang on to her; that Chloe's love and determination would win the day. The accident at the PC Rally when Chloe fell off and Martini caught her face with a flying hoof still haunts me, but as she said, "Just because I fell off and got a black eye doesn't mean to say I don't still love Martini and want to give up riding." Brave little girl, but I understand because, of course, I've felt the same about Bella.

SEPTEMBER 5TH

Hooray! Today I hitched up and harrowed completely alone. I long-reined Bella round the field a few times and then positioned her by the harrow. She looked a little twitchy so I produced a tit-bit to give her something else to think about while I hitched the left rein on the hame and walked round the back with the right and hooked on the trace chain. If she'd moved at that point I'd have been in trouble, but she didn't so I went back round the front throwing the reins over and popping another titbit in her mouth on the way. There was a tricky moment when she started to move off before I'd moved back and gathered up both reins but she soon stopped. Her head jerked up when she realised I'd hitched her up and for an awful moment I thought she was going to wheel round, but with a tweak on the right rein she set off and soon settled down. I was so thrilled I could have marched up and down the field all day, but I quit after about ten minutes while she was still all sweetness and light. Again, a vulnerable moment while I unhitched and she moved off a bit sooner than I meant but I succeeded! I've learned enough about this horsebreaking business now, not to be fooled into thinking it will go so well every time, but to have done it once – to have harnessed, hitched up, harrowed and unhitched all without mishap or mayhem is absolutely fantastic.

SEPTEMBER 10TH

I got straight into the cart and Bella soon settled into plodding round the field. I'm having difficulties though in keeping her body straight in the shafts. I suggested to Diane that perhaps she drive next time; my inexperience coupled with Bella's is probably not helping. Diane told me she'd bumped into Gilbert who'd asked how I was getting on and how he must come down here and see for himself. But... he insisted he could only come when Q was here in case people got the wrong idea! Diane and I collapsed with laughter at the thought of me and Gilbert getting up to something! Gilbert is small and sinewy with a broken-toothed grin that cracks his face in two, coupled with the most lecherous twinkle I've ever seen. But I don't think he's quite my type...

SEPTEMBER 11TH

William has suddenly gone lame so I called Crispin. He's got a septic toe which apparently is quite common in donkeys. Poor William - he looks so unhappy. I have to clean and spray the hole each day and plug it with cotton wool. Rather William than Bella! We discussed Bella's problem foot and I showed him the pictures. He said we may have to resort to general anaesthetic to treat it properly, in which case we need to know whether she's in foal or not. Crispin took some blood which was no mean feat in itself. It can't really have hurt her and yet she nearly flattened us both quite deliberately. Crispin believes that we'll always be plagued with foot problems, living on marshland. Certainly neither William nor Humphrey ever had a single problem with their feet when we lived at Paddock Hall.

Over coffee afterwards, Crispin gave Chloe a syringe

(without needle) and explained the fun of trying to shoot down your toes with water in the bath. What a talented vet I have...

SEPTEMBER 13TH

It was one of those magical autumn mornings: a brisk September chill in the air but the sky a beautiful duck egg blue. Bob Bussingham came. First he showed me the simple way to put the hames on: turn the collar upside down and fasten the hames at the bottom before turning it the right way up. No more stretching and struggling, no more standing on tiptoe stretching both arms round her neck; no more accidentally dropping the hames on her foot. It's so simple when you know how. He also let the bottom latch out a bit so that the points of the hames come higher. Then we put on the trace harness. No wonder it had slipped back. We hadn't got the chains or straps in the right place at all. Then I put the bridle on and Bob pointed out that I'd got it too high so that she could see out of the bottom of the blinkers. So we let it down a hole. He doesn't like the Liverpool bit and suggests I try a straight one that hooks on one side. But he understood my point that the brakes of the Liverpool bit give me confidence. He was horrified at the tangled mess of lines – said to take them off each time and showed me how to loop them neatly like cat's cradle. Throughout all this Bella stood quietly as anything. Bob was clearly impressed and I was proud – and surprised! Then Bob asked me to long-rein her round the field and told me to stand at the back rather than the side for better control. Finally he thinned her tail (he agrees with keeping them long) and showed me how to tie it up for winter work. His fingers worked so fast and nimbly that I suspect I shall have problems when I come to try it! I learned so much this morning – I just wish I'd contacted him earlier. His general verdict on Bella: "She'll be a nice mare when she's five or six. Pity she's so jumpy though. What you should have got was a working horse that somebody wanted a good home for." I agreed heartily but pointed out that people keep good working horses – they only sell the problem or inexperienced ones.

SEPTEMBER 14TH

I should have gone to work today but it was a misty morning, hinting at another superb autumn day to come in an hour or two. I was itching to try out all Bob's advice and so I decided to hell with work. Bella was in a delicious mood: peaceful, relaxed, quiet. Just as well since I had an awful struggle with the trace harness. I thought the cart harness was heavy enough but this really seems to weigh a ton. After several attempts, I finally managed to throw the lot over her back and then sort out what went where. I long-reined round the field for a few minutes and she seemed so relaxed that I decided to hitch on the harrow without further ado. Bob's way is so much simpler – and safer. None of that potentially dangerous running round the front of her. We moved off a little before I was ready and I discovered I'd got the right line inside the chains but I decided it was better to keep going. She took quite a while to settle down, pulling hard at the lines but eventually she resigned herself to the job in hand. By the time we finished she was sweating nicely. I gave us both a big pat on the back. "One woman went to harrow, went to harrow a meadow. One woman and her horse, went to harrow a meadow".

SEPTEMBER 15TH

I dropped Chloe off at the Puppet Club to be collected by

Hannah's mother, and headed for Barway Farm, Doddington and the auction of the Jolley Collection. Nearly 1,000 lots ranging from old Fenland hand tools to vintage tractors – and a crowd with money to match. Prices were sky high, certainly no bargains to be had. There were 23 single furrow ploughs as well as various two and three furrow ploughs, ridging and lifting ploughs. Stan Hammond and Gilbert Edwards were there (the latter admitted he'd rung to ask for a lift but I'd already left – what of the gossips??) Both took me in hand and agreed a Ransomes Model SHP plough was the best for me. Stan reckoned £50 while Gilbert thought £70 should be absolutely top whack. I asked Stan to bid for me and to go to £75. It made £95, in fact over £100 when you add VAT and 5% buyer's premium. I'm glad Stan bid for me: I'd probably have ended up buying it for well over £100, left to my own devices and desires! I was horrified to find that Stan had sold a chain harrow for £25 last week. If only I'd thought to tell him that I wanted one. A Lister Blackstone swath turner went for a mere £12 – I was tempted but looking at that vulnerable seat just above those revolving spokes, I decided I'd be better with a tractor drawn turner behind the cart. I was chuffed to see a Huxtable hay rake – vastly inferior to mine - make £170. Prices were indeed crazy. I left empty handed but didn't feel too bad as Stan and Gilbert have promised to help me find a plough at a better price.

SEPTEMBER 21ST

I did wonder whether working was a good idea today: a single magpie on the drive and a very strong wind keening across the marshes. Especially since I didn't do so well on Wednesday when she pranced and backed a little too much for comfort. But nothing ventured, nothing broken, and so I loaded on the harness and hitched up. It was not a promising start. She veered sharply to the left so that I had to move the harrows round, and then she stepped back on to them. Finally she seemed to accept the situation and we plodded up and down very steadily. Now and then she gave the odd jump, whether it was the wind up her tail or the rough ground, I don't know. I worked her for twenty minutes; it would be nice to keep increasing that time without stepping over the boredom threshold and ending on a sour note.

SEPTEMBER 23RD

Another good, satisfying harrow despite a minor tantrum to start with which meant I had to unhitch and start again. Thirty minutes today and by the end we were crisscrossing the field as through we'd done it for years. Paul Heiney writes about how his concentration wanders during harrowing and of course that famous Thomas Hardy poem "In Time of The Breaking of Nations" echoes that idea:

Only a man harrowing clods
In a slow silent walk
with an old horse that stumbles and nods
Half asleep as they stalk
Only thin smoke without flame
from the heaps of couch-grass
Yet this will go onward the same
Though dynasties pass

But I can't see it myself. I think there is an extraordinary skill in driving your horse in a straight line, exactly along the mark of the previous line. You can't see it sometimes until you're almost on it and so you go back and forth with the feeling that either you're going over the same ground or missing out vast chunks. Certainly you can't do it half asleep! Bella's mouth is so sensitive that I know it's me rather than her, who's over-controlling and hence doing a kind of drunken zig zag. Last workout for a week probably as I'm on a farm ops course at the Clarks' Weylands Farm next week.

SEPTEMBER 24TH

1 pm: I arrive to register as instructed, to find the other three have been there since 9 am, although they shouldn't have been. We attempted to put a roll together (it was some time before I realised what it was, I'd no idea they were made up of separate rings) and then it was time for lunch which is all included in the £180. Roast chicken, roast potatoes, cauliflower and bread sauce followed by fruit pie and custard. Well worth it for the food alone! On the course are Maggie and her husband Bob who live in Leicester and are moving to a 350 acre farm in Scotland, intending to work it with two Suffolks and a Clydesdale. They seem frightfully well organised and efficient, having gleaned all their knowledge from every book ever written rather than hands-on experience. The third member is Richard who used to work two Shires in Shropshire and is now at the Gressenhall Rural Life Museum, hoping to start breaking two three year-old Suffolks soon. We finished lunch, Roger reminded us about steel-capped boots and then it was time for me to race back to Norwich to collect Chloe while the others harnessed up and set to work. Frustrating – but that's the joys of motherhood! Before I left, I showed Roger Clark the pictures of Bella's foot. He and Cheryl are both convinced that it is canker. They say it needs cutting off completely by hobbling her and pulling her down on to the yard. "Don't let them give her a general anaesthetics," they warned. "Heavy horses don't have strong hearts and all too often they don't come round." Roger offered to do the job if Crispin or Mark aren't willing.

Started giving hay tonight. It was greeted with immense enthusiasm, but the four of them didn't finish off the half bale I put out.

Good news and bad news tonight. I had a long chat with Crispin. He agrees with Roger that canker is probably the problem with Bella and that the only remedy is to cut right back to the quick, fit a special shoe and treat it with antibiotics. However, he disagrees with Roger about how to do it: he feels that a general anaesthetic is the only way to do the job. That is possible since luckily the pregnancy test has proved negative. The good news is that Stan Hammond rang to say that he's found me a plough for £60. Chloe and I will collect it on Sunday before going to the Autumn Working.

SEPTEMBER 25TH

We set to ploughing today with Samba and Noble. Roger showed us how to measure out, starting some four or five yards from the edge of the field, skimming first and then keeping the furrow wheel firmly against the edge of the furrow wall. With horses like those two it wasn't nearly as difficult as I'd imagined, but then those two horses know exactly what they're doing. It's fantastic to hear Roger mutter "Get in the furrow Sam" and see that great Percheron obediently sidestep his huge feet into the right place, or he says "Just try it" and the horse takes one measured step. A surprisingly light touch was needed on the plough handles and turning at the end was much easier than I'd thought too. You make the horses do all the work, leaning the plough on its back (i.e. the left) rather than on the breast. "The aim," said Roger, "is to keep the surface level." No wonder he put us to plough in a field that couldn't be seen from the road! It was a thrilling experience; if you've never walked the furrow behind a pair of horses you simply haven't lived. The experience defies description. I can't wait to try with Bella but Roger advises first that I lead her in the furrow, then long-rein in the furrow (apparently they often try to walk anywhere but in the furrow) and then pull a log along the furrow – several times before actually attaching the plough. That all seems to make good sense - I'm glad I didn't just launch into the field with Bella plus plough in my usual cavalier way.

SEPTEMBER 26TH

A three horse team today: Noble, Samba and Turpin. The three white Percherons made a magnificent sight as they worked their way steadily across the reddish sandy earth with an autumnal blue sky as the backdrop. We started off cultivating, then tried the Cambridge roll with Roger pointing out the importance of using shafts or some form of brake on rising land as there is no way you could stop a roll from crashing into the horses' hocks downhill. We worked in pairs taking turns to drive the horses and steer the roll, resulting in some very decorative wavy lines.

SEPTEMBER 27TH

We hitched up Samba and Noble to two carts and set off along the road to load hay. It was interesting to see how reluctant the normally angelic Sam was to leave home. We loaded an amazing amount of hay on to the carts, only to discover that one was too high to get out of the barn door! But by adjusting the back chain and leaning on the shafts we managed to get it out. As we walked the horses back to Weylands, I tried to squeeze some tips out of Cheryl on how to put a young horse to a cart on your own. She wasn't very helpful: "You'll just have to get help." But I persevered, and eventually she suggested letting one shaft hang on the collar while you go round to do the other one - but checking first that the horse doesn't mind the twisting effect on the collar while someone is nearby. We unloaded the hay, had another huge delicious lunch (I've put on a horrendous amount of weight this week) before hooking the horses up to the harrows. As Roger said, "Anyone can keep two good horses like those straight in the furrow, but the real skill is in driving a straight line." And it's not nearly as easy as it looks even with horses like Samba and Noble. It made me feel much better about my wandering lines with Bella. Cheryl told me to practise not only going in a straight line, but stopping at the very edge, turning, stopping and then going back again. "Put their heads in the hedge and then if they have a munch they'll want to come back the next time," she chuckled. But my fields are hedgeless!

SEPTEMBER 28TH

Sadly the last day of what has been an interesting and informative week. Well worth the money. We finished off harrowing the first field and started on a second. We're all getting better at keeping straight and turning, although Maggie managed to overturn the harrows. If they do overturn you'd have quite a job on your own to unhook and throw them the right way up, as well as hanging on to the horse. After lunch (quiche and the lightest of steamed treacle puddings) we put Sam with Noble in trace harness to the trolley but I had to miss any more in order to get back to Norwich. It was a beautiful evening, light until about 7 pm, and so I put on Bella's bridle with no harness and long-reined her across the field, stopping at the very edge, turning and stopping again. To my amazement, she took it really well. The perfect end to an excellent week and a first class way of working off all those delicious steamed puddings.

September 30th

Chloe and I towed the trailer over to Stan Hammond and picked up my plough. The furrow wheel seems to be immovable but hopefully some heat will help. I chatted to Stan about Bella's foot; he'd never heard of heavy horses having problems with anaesthetics and suggested I contact a horse vet at King's Lynn for a third opinion. Then we dashed back to the Autumn Working at Scoulton. We bumped into Gressenhall Richard with his wife May and after nattering away there was only time for a brief look at the horses before the heavens opened and obliterated the rest of the day. It was a slow drive home, what with the trailer and floods of water on the roads.

October 1st

Drama indeed! I pegged out the washing, filled the buckets and did a head count, as always, on the river bank. I could see Martini, William and Humphrey but no Bella. Then to my horror, I saw a black and white face poking out of the reeds in the dyke. I found her stuck fast in the mud, very frightened and very tired. I put the halter on and tried to encourage her out but it was obviously no use. The Loddon fire crew arrived just 10 minutes after my 999 call, followed 20 minutes later by the Beccles engine. As they waded, dug, pulled and sweated, Bella grew visibly more exhausted. As she lay with her head on the bank and eyes closed it was apparent that she had given up. I really thought it was going to be Friday all over again. Since most of her massive body was concealed in the mud, I tried to explain to the firemen how big she was. I don't think they believed me until, two hours after they arrived, they succeeded in hauling her out of the dyke. I've never seen men move back so fast as she stood there, stunned with shock, cold and exhaustion, dripping with mud. They kindly offered to hose off the mud, but I thought that was adding insult to injury and so I led her to the yard and gave her a bran mash while Chloe and I dried her as well as we could with hay. She still seemed so cold and shivery that I made her another bran mash and put an old blanket over her. Fortunately it was a lovely sunny morning – it could have been fatal if it had been wet and windy – and I walked her round and round the field to get her circulation moving. Some two hours later I could feel her warming up so I put Martini in with her for company and took Chloe to school. (At least she had one of the more original excuses for being late!) In the evening Bella seemed none the worse for her ordeal, but I thought another bran mash would do no harm.

OCTOBER 2ND

Incredibly, less than 24 hours after being hauled from a watery grave, Bella was pulling the cart. Despite the time gap since she was last in shafts, she pulled slowly and steadily. Next time, up the drive.

OCTOBER 4TH

It was a lovely morning, and so I decided to show off to Mummy who had never seen me working with Bella. For once, we had no messing about to start with (I gave her a bit more head as Diane suggested I may have been holding her back too much to start with. I think it's called beginner's panic!) and then went backwards and forwards as though we'd done it for years, dutifully stopping at the edge, turning and stopping again. I felt so proud of us both! On Stan's advice I rang his horse vet today and he said he'd never heard of there being a problem and couldn't see why there should be. "Of course if you over-dose them they won't wake up," he said, "but personally I can't see any reason for giving a horse a general anaesthet-ic anyway if the work is external." He explained that he would much rather sedate the horse and then nerve block the foot so that she felt no pain. "But she'd have to be sen-sible enough to stand on three feet and not jump about." Is Bella sensible enough? Oh help, now I have three differ-ent options: dope and pull down, general anaesthetic, nerve block and standing up. I shall have to ring Crispin again.

OCTOBER 9TH

We drove Bella and the cart up the drive today. She was a little kangarooish to start with because it is so bumpy but then we settled. It was a little tricky turning at the yellow gate, but we managed it and came back very nicely. Next time I shall drive up the drive or round the field on my own. Wilbur came too, as usual. Bella seems perfectly happy to see him criss-crossing in front of her or leaping out of the dyke in pursuit of a pheasant. It's a pity the other two aren't so sensible - Orville is frightened of Bella and tends to rush at her, barking, while Sam is just too mad for words.

I have spoken to Crispin who agreed to humour me and try sedation on the yard, but he would obviously prefer a general anaesthetic. Plans are under way to fence off the yard this weekend for the safety of us all.

OCTOBER 13TH

Another milestone: I drove Bella in the cart today alone for the first time. I hitched her in all right (letting the collar twist as Cheryl suggested), leapt aboard and, mindful of Diane's advice, asked her to walk on with a loose rein. Walk on? To my horror we set off at a cracking pace but she soon calmed down and so did I – and we walked steadily round the field. Then I saw the fencing man coming down the drive so I stopped before I'd have liked to, and while hurrying to unhitch her, did my back in. I was suddenly in dire agony and reaching up to remove her collar nearly proved an insurmountable problem. The lesson today is clear: never hurry. My recurrent back problems date back to the day when I fell out of a hot air balloon and broke my neck. I do seriously wonder whether I'm fit enough, young enough, strong enough to have a horse like Bella.

OCTOBER 29TH

Diane came today, and we drove Bella in the cart up the drive. I say "we" – i.e. I sat in the cart and drove while Diane kept pace alongside on the lungeline. We went well and turned nicely at the yellow gate - Bella showing us that she's much better at backing and filling without our interference. For practice, we made her stop on the way back, near the pump house, and she threw a tantrum, backing me and the cart at a horrifying rate back up the drive. Not a nice feeling. I suppose the only way to stop her is to touch her with the whip (which I didn't have with me), although I then run the risk of her bolting or going up. Eventually we stopped – luckily just before the corner – and I made her stop several times more on the way home.

My back was agony afterwards – although I have been successfully managing to harrow during the past week.

NOVEMBER 2ND

A good 30 minutes' harrowing today with Bella's head well down leaning properly into the collar. In the evening I rang Mike Flood and bought a flat roll for £20. We chatted about cart-horses in general and Bella in particular – "keep the reins low down in line with her mouth" was his handy advice. He told me how he'd had one who took off and he'd held on with one rein so that it went round and round in circles. "When it was dizzy and wanted to stop, I made it go on. We must have done it for half an hour. She didn't run off after that," he added triumphantly. He also told me how he's had horses in the dyke and that he now has all his marshes fenced off. I shall order electric fencing tomorrow, I simply can't go through that awful experience again.

NOVEMBER 6TH

After weighing up the pros and cons of the various options, Mark has decided to try and do Bella's foot alone – without Crispin or nerve blocks. He worked his way as usual through Martini, William and Humphrey before coming to Bella. Then he cut away about 80% of the diseased part – rather than trying her patience and going for 100%. She stood extraordinarily quietly, bearing in mind the complete lack of painkillers or nerve blocks, and only gave the odd violent swing when Mark pressed in the iodine and sugar mixture. He then packed in strips of old T-towels, before putting on the shoe and screwing the plate in place. She looks a bit lop-footed now with one foot eerily clanking on the yard, but it doesn't seem to worry her at all. I'm so pleased I decided on Mark doing it and that he decided against Crispin's help. Bella trusts Mark and if anybody can do it without anaesthetics, he's the only one. If she'd gone to Roger Clark and he'd pulled her down on to their yard, she'd never have forgotten the experience and it's Mark and I who would have suffered afterwards. Mind, when I told Mark Roger had offered to do it, I was amused that he turned to me in amazement and asked why I hadn't agreed. Shame on you, Mark, I said, I thought you'd enjoy the challenge! The only problem is, I'm meant to change the dressing at least every other day, but Mark and I are agreed it really is an impossible task for me on my own. So he is going to try and fit in coming back to do it for me as often as he can. Bella is very lucky to have such a lovely farrier.

NOVEMBER 7TH

Today was a good example of how so many things can go wrong in such a short space of time. It was such a golden morning, once the early mist had cleared the marshes, that I decided to try the cart. As usual Bella stood quietly while I harnessed up and then led her to the cart. She tried her customary sidestep out of the shafts, but the temptation of a peppermint persuaded her to back properly. I hitched up with no problems at all, got in and moved off a little sooner than I meant, but in a reasonably controlled manner. We plodded round the field and then I noticed that the right front tug was dangling loose. So I stopped, got out and did it up again. I then got back in and tried to move off, but Bella thought she'd done enough. She started backing, so I yelled and growled at her and eventually, with very bad grace, she moved jerkily off. Then the wanty came undone. Before I could stop her, she'd trodden on the end of it and unnerved herself by being hauled up short. So I got out again, tied it up and got back in. This time Bella was convinced she'd had enough. We started moving backwards at an alarming rate of knots towards the dyke. Fearing a soaking, I leapt out and stopped her, inches from the edge. I told her to walk on and she took another step back, so I touched her lightly with the whip. Wow! Anyone would think I'd put a red hot poker up her backside. Up she went (thank heavens the wanty was done up) and then she attempted to take off. I prayed that I wouldn't let go and for once God must have taken pity on my plight, because I held on. We then had several more exciting minutes of rearing, prancing and plunging before continuing in a fast and somewhat unsteady walk. I was just about to get in for the third time when I noticed that the front tug had come undone again. So we called it a day - a rather unsuccessful one at that. Bella was covered in sweat; she'd certainly given herself a fright as well as me, but at least I'd held on and we were both in one piece. In this game, you learn to be thankful for very small mercies. The wanty came undone because of my knot, but I don't understand why the front tug came unattached – twice. As far as I know, I didn't do anything different.

NOVEMBER 9TH

Luckily Bella hasn't taken umbrage after Wednesday's fiasco. She backed fairly happily between the shafts before we set off up the drive. We passed the yellow gate reluctantly on Bella's part as she thinks that's her turning place – and turned very neatly in a gateway further up. We stopped several times on the way back, but there was no attempt to reverse. A good morning's work and she certainly earned her bucketful today. I can only think that I didn't have the tug chain in the right link because there were certainly no problems today.

Bella shows how neatly she can turn the cart on the track

November 10th

Richard from Gressenhall came today. Bella was very wary of him at first: who was this strange man smelling of pigs? But his quiet, gentle manner soon reassured her. We decided to try her in the cart in the field, rather than up the drive as this was to be her first time driven by someone other than me or Diane. Richard was impressed at how quietly and patiently she stood but she let me down as soon as we tried to move off. She backed and plunged and rebelled. "Is she always like this?" asked a rather shaken Richard. I assured him no, only sometimes. Then he got in the cart while I took the lunge line and she moved off properly and after a little while I got in as well. Richard thought her mouth was lovely, he couldn't believe how readily she responds to just the merest vibration of the fingers. "That's what they mean when they talk about driving a horse on a piece of cotton." He congratulated me on doing a good job which was heart-warming to hear. He also thought she looked really fit and healthy and that the short feed she's having is obviously going upwards rather than outwards. He's not feeding his Suffolks at all, apart from hay. Mark came in the afternoon to change the dressing and again Richard was impressed by Bella's forbearance, to say nothing of Mark's! The old T-towel strips smelt vile, strangely acrid and much worse than that distinctive thrush smell.

November 12th

The marsh was shrouded in a dense fog that didn't lift all day. Despite the permeating dampness, I love living here on days like this. The marsh is quiet at any time, but the fog blankets out every sound – even the ducks are hushed

- and I revel in the idea that there is no one else in the world. I never know loneliness, only solitude. I didn't see why Bella should mind the fog, so we set off in the cart. She went really well except I made the mistake of trying to turn her in a part of the drive that Bella obviously thought was too narrow. She did her usual backing and filling to turn – and suddenly I was sitting in the cart in the dyke! I leapt out, went to her head and encouraged her to pull the cart out of the water. Once we were back on the track again, I jumped back in and dripped my way home.

November 30th

Another first today: Bella plus cart on the road for the first time. Her one metal foot made a lovely clanking on the hard road quite unlike the usual soft unshod sound. She did well, despite that wretched old fool Wright deliberately trying to spook her, a bicycle, some men working on a house and a van squeezing past her. She seemed extra-sensitive on her mouth, twice putting in a couple of bucks and when we got back one side of her gum was red. Diane thinks the bit has slipped down a little. She was certainly tired out by the time we returned; she stood between the shafts with her nose nearly touching the ground. But she soon brightened up when she saw her bucket filled with Quiet Mix, pulp, maize, barley and carrots. I don't seem to have filled in this diary for a while; perhaps because I've been working her two or three times a week and there's been nothing spectacular to report. Thank God, since spectacular happenings tend to be disasters! Sometimes she's lovely; sometimes she's too full of herself, perhaps because of the sudden cold turn in the weather, or maybe just bloody-mindedness. I suppose she really is broken now; all we both need is practice and experience. Mark is still trying to come twice a week to re-stuff her foot with the paste and rags. It's no worse but not actually any better. Mark is going to talk to Crispin; perhaps the wetness that seeps in – which we can't prevent - is slowing down the healing process. If it really needs to be kept bone-dry I shall have problems. The only way would be to keep all of them on the yard – or at least let Martini and the donkeys take it in turns to keep her company. Soon I will have had Bella two years. I would so like to have put a plough behind her so I can feel she really is broken to chains, shafts and plough.

DECEMBER 14TH

We put Bella to the plough for the very first time today. It had been a disastrous start to the morning with personal and business problems and Diane was worried that I was too wound up to try something new. But I need Bella for relaxation. Some people play golf, others watch television, but my escape from the pressures of people and running a flying school is to 'play' with Bella. I am at my happiest when my horse and I are alone on the marsh, working in tune with each other. So I knew today that Bella was just what I needed. To start with, we long-reined her along the bank a couple of times before hooking on the plough. Diane held her head while I took the lines and she accepted it remarkably well, despite nearly mowing Diane down. But after all our effort all you could see in the ground was hoofprints and the merest trace of a line! Not only does the plough need adjusting but so does the harness as it kept slipping back like it did before with the harrow. Bob Bussingham's help is obviously a necessity. But it was a start - and an exciting one.

DECEMBER 28TH

Mark came to do Bella's foot as usual on Christmas Eve and I told him that I thought I ought to have a go at it. Partly because I think it needs treating more frequently than Mark is able to do, and also because I can't afford his visits, reasonable though they undoubtedly are. So instead of holding Bella's head as I usually do, I sat at the back and watched the whole process while Mark explained the importance of not getting my finger trapped under the shoe while pushing in the rags. I had intended to have a go on Boxing Day, but it was a wild, wet day and I felt it would be folly. Yesterday was out as I was working and so I set to today. I propped her foot on the straw bale as I need two hands to undo the fiddly bolts, and Bella was surprisingly patient as I grunted and groaned. I took out the stinking wet rags, cleaned the foot out with hydrogen peroxide and then packed in the iodine and sugar. She started to fidget then. Crispin swears that the mixture doesn't sting but I do wonder since she always objects to that more than anything else. Then I re-packed with clean rags, cleaned the plate and attempted to bolt it back on. Easier said than done! The bolts are tiny and Bella only has to move her foot slightly on the bale and they're gone. I lost one completely and then Bella got fed up. I fiddled away and at last got one bolt in. I let her foot go for a bit to give us both a rest before summoning up the strength to put the remaining four bolts in. What a performance! The last time Mark came, he told me that the chap who makes the bolts for him had asked whether it was a big, beefy bloke who owned the horse. "No, she's a very sweet (sic), small lady" said Mark. The chap was horrified – as well he might be! But once the back-breaking work was done, we went for a ride up the drive with Chloe in the cart for the first time. I made Chloe wear her riding hat – just in case – but Bella was good as gold, and Chloe adored her first cart ride. Chloe and Bella have an extraordinarily close relationship. Bella will often stand quietly for Chloe when she won't for me; perhaps she recognises a kindred sprit.

DECEMBER 29TH

My horoscope today said "There is no doubt whatsoever that you have a very difficult furrow to plough..." Never were truer words spoken. The day started with Wilbur having a fit. I held him while he shook for about 10 minutes. Then he seemed to recover, but while I was feeding the ducks he suddenly went mad, screaming and running full tilt in circles. He crashed into Goosey (our Chinese goose who thinks he's a duck) and then fell headlong into the river.

He hauled himself out and then ran round the field, still screaming. It was appalling. I felt quite sick with fear and helplessness. While Chloe listened out for the vet to return my call, I tackled Bella's foot. Those bolts will be my undoing. I've lost another and the only way I could get them back in was to enlist Chloe's help. She did a song and dance act to keep Bella amused while I struggled to screw the plate back in. The trouble is that compared with Mark, I'm so slow and Bella simply gets bored with the whole process. And trying to screw fiddly little bolts into a swinging foot is not the easiest job in the world. Oh, animals!

JANUARY 4TH

My beloved Wilbur was put to sleep. I cradled his head in my arms as the needle slid into his leg, but I don't think he even knew I was there.

January 6th

To Chloe's delight, we are snowed in! I think this must be the first snow Bella has ever seen because she was so funny with it. Her brow wrinkled in amazement as she snorted into the strange white stuff and found it blew up her nostrils and into her eyes. Martini, meanwhile, just took it all in her stride, pawing the ground to get at the grass. Poor Orville and Sam have the type of hair that forms snowballs all along their tummies and legs so that eventually they can't move until they thaw out! The river is completely frozen so in the mornings the ducks and geese perform a graceful ballet as they slither across to us for food. Chloe is in seventh heaven and praying that it lasts for weeks. I have to admit that it looks very beautiful, unsullied by vehicles and humans.

January 11th

What with Christmas, Wilbur's death and the snow and then gales, I have been feeling drained and listless, letting Bella have a long break. And as if that wasn't enough, my marriage has finally expired and I find myself with one daughter, two horses, two donkeys, two dogs, two sheep, one rabbit, chickens and a mortgage to support – with no reliable income. Can I really afford to keep Bella? I decided to cheer myself up by galvanising Bella into action for a long-rein trip up the drive and along the road. I negotiated the gate rather neatly on the way out I thought, and the drive presented no real problems – just a gentle touch with the whip now and then to keep her moving on. At the top of the drive a tractor and trailer loaded with hay passed and I thought how lucky I'd been to have missed that, and turned into the road only to confront a second one. I

Bella, Martini and William enjoy the snow — a first for Bella

turned Bella back into the drive and circled her until it moved on. We did fine then, with a couple of cars and a bicycle passing us, until a flock of sheep suddenly appeared in the gateway. Before I could stop her Bella had swung round for home – one moment I was looking at her backside, the next we were face to face - but I hung on and forced her round again to continue walking on. We only continued a short way before turning when unfortunately she caught her foot on the verge which gave her another fright. On the way back, an enormous lorry came up behind us and so I steered Bella on to the verge before beckoning him to pass us. Bella obviously knew he was there, but not until his wing mirror suddenly popped up three inches from her blinkers did she realise how close he was. Up she went in terror and there was a second when she could have raced for home. But again I hung on and we let the lorry pass before venturing back into the road and continuing for home at a cracking pace. The relief of turning into the drive and feeling we were home (despite another two miles to go) was enormous. We'd survived and I felt really cheered. I'm relatively happy long-reining her alone on the road for traffic practice but I think it would be madness to take the cart out on my own yet. At least I've got a few miles of drive to play with for solo trips.

January 22nd

It's about three weeks since we went out in the cart, but Bella backed in readily, even doing the neatest bit of side-stepping with her front feet to get between the shafts that I've ever seen. Talk about a pro! She then pulled steadily and happily up the drive. We went a short way along the road and met a lorry loaded with pallets. Bella was not impressed, although the driver very kindly pulled in and switched off. She refused to go on, so I got out and coaxed her past. We turned back sooner than we meant having spotted a workman's pipe lying across the road. After all, there are limits to Bella's tolerance and bravery. So we turned in rather too narrow a part of the road with Bella having to push the cart hard back into the verge. But she managed it, albeit with a second or two of panic as she realised that she couldn't back any more and her metal foot slipped on the tarmac. But we coped.

JANUARY 26TH

I went to Mike Flood's to collect the single horse roll today. Not the best of starts: I'd got two miles along the road when some alarm started off in the car. I found that the trailer had fused my lights, so I continued, but with no trailer lights – and right through the centre of Norwich with lots of police around for the football! I got there eventually and Mike loaded everything in – the roller, axle, shafts etc. I just hope I can put it all together now. But for £20 it seems a good deal. Mike was very friendly and helpful and we chatted for a long time in the bitter cold of a raw January afternoon. Mike's a real Norfolk 'bor' who works and shows his Shires when earning his living allows him time. He first harrowed a horse at the age of seven and used to harness up by standing in the manger because he was too small to reach up! He thought I'd probably got the draught line of the chains wrong with the plough and that we need to lower the hooks on the hip straps. Then the collar won't be pulled up and back.

I left him much too late because I needed lights straight away and so with some trepidation I traversed Norwich, staying clear of the football ground, and arrived home without incident.

January 29th

Diane came for the last time for a while since I am broke and we took Bella and cart up the drive and through Langley. It was interesting to see that as soon as she passed out of her familiar territory, her apprehension increased. Some concrete bollards nearly proved impassable, and then it was binbags, the village sign - oh so many new and different sights. To say nothing of smells: we had to pass a barn full of pigs which she could smell and hear but not see. It's funny how horses generally don't seem to like pigs, although Roger Clark swears that his horses don't seem to mind black pigs nearly as much as the pink variety. Racist horses?

Including the drive, we must have covered a good six miles and so we were all tired and sweaty by the time we returned.

* * *

Well, two years have passed since Bella arrived, reluctant filly that she was. Two years of traumas and triumphs – but we have emerged relatively unscathed. I don't know which of us has undergone the greater transformation. Certainly, I find it difficult to recall just how inexperienced, raw and frightened I was. And I suppose the same could be said of Bella. I can't boast that she's 100% perfect, by any means, and she may never be. For instance, she still moves off too quickly in the cart, tosses her head so violently out of the bridle that she jars her mouth and I'm mindful of the danger that one day she may take off again. I shall never be able to trust her completely but perhaps that's no bad thing: at least I'll never be complacent! But she is not yet four, in real years, and we have a long way to go together. Sadly, we're still battling with the canker in her foot, but even there we've made progress. It is getting better, albeit slowly, but the cool, calm way she lets both Mark and me pick up her feet now is a joy. Incredible to think that at one time I wondered whether I'd ever be able to pick up her feet at all – and now I unbolt and bolt the plate back on without turning a hair! I suspect we will always have foot problems of some sort or another due to the continuation of the deep clefts in her foot and living on marshland.

Bella and I have had a week's holiday at the Clarks. Cheryl had obviously forgotten her advice about shooting her – and I didn't jog her memory – but when I reminded her that I'd broken her she looked less than enthusiastic. But amazingly, throughout the week Bella never put a foot wrong. We drove her round the narrow Suffolk lanes in Cheryl's hitchcart meeting tractors, lorries, irrigation sprays and pigs to name but a few everyday hazards, and Bella never let me down. In the mornings she stood quietly in her stall alongside Samba before setting out for a day's work, like the true professionals. It was a marvellous week and when Cheryl commented that I'd done a good job I was over the moon. Praise from the top indeed! I know that this is just a beginning, that now Bella and I both have to gain experience and confidence but, hopefully, the hard work is done, although I'm sure there are lots of surprises in store for us.

The question is: Would I do it again, knowing what I know now? The answer has to be no.

It is possible for a complete ignoramus to break a carthorse – I've proved it – but it is definitely not the ideal way. With the benefit of that marvellous thing called hindsight, I realise that I should have bought a well-broken working horse. The problem is, there are very few really good working horses for sale; understandably, because a 12 to 16 year old good worker represents years of effort that are, quite simply, priceless. There are plenty of recent-

A working horse at last. . . Bella brings in the hay

ly broken four or five year olds around, but they are not suitable for the novice. So the only remaining alternative is to buy a two year old and have it broken professionally. There are many people around who will do this - some are better than others. You miss out on the bruises this way, but also the satisfaction. Because, it has to be said, there is nothing quite so exhilarating as working a horse you have broken yourself. During the whole exhausting process, Bella and I have learned so much about each other that we now read each other's minds and moods. People suggest there is some mystique about breaking a horse. I don't believe there is, but it does require experience, time and patience and a certain amount of courage. You should be able to break a horse in a matter of weeks: it took me two years.

There is a growing interest in heavy horses, especially working models; not working the land economically but, like Bella, doing a little now and then as a sort of hobby horse. And to cater for us newcomers, there are lots of courses and associations to supply help and advice. I would recommend any would-be heavy horse owner does the groundwork first – this diary should convince of the folly of doing anything else! There are still lots of old horsemen around whose knowledge is invaluable – getting it out of them is quite another matter!

I've been lucky with Bella but I wouldn't tempt fate by trying to repeat the experience. She has been broken, despite my efforts, and now that we have survived to tell the tale I wouldn't part with her for the world.

But do it again? You must be joking!

THE END

Real life, unlike fiction, does not always produce a happy ending.

Six years on, the chance to make a fresh start in Northumberland arose but property prices in the North East meant that, even with the money from the flying school I could not afford to buy a house and sufficient land for Bella to work. And so, reluctantly, I decided to let her go on permanent loan to somebody who would work her or breed from her. I refused to sell her as I wanted to safeguard her future; she was after all, still a relative youngster. This way, I could remove her at any time if I felt she was unhappy.

There was a surprisingly good response to my advertisement in Heavy Horse World, but I rejected most of them on the telephone for one reason or another. Three people came to see Bella, and she decided, in her inimitable way, to reject two of them. I wasn't worried: she didn't have to go as we had not yet finalised sale and purchase. I felt it was down to Fate: Bella would go only if we found the perfect home for her and if we managed to find someone crazy enough to buy The Round House.

Both Bella and I liked the last family to answer the advertisement. They had a 40 acre farm in North Yorkshire (just two hours down the road from Northumberland), a horse-mad daughter of Chloe's age and K— seemed a genuinely kind and caring potential "owner." Chloe and I visited the farm and decided that Bella really had fallen on her feet.

I worked her one last time in the field and to add to my heartbreak, she behaved impeccably. The following day she left for Yorkshire and Chloe and I cried our eyes out. Over the next year I visited Bella frequently and was upset to find that they were not working her as I had hoped. The horse-mad daughter had discovered that fun comes on two legs rather than four, and I got the impression that Bella had frightened K—. Her feet were untrimmed, her coat had lost its sheen and her mane and tail were tangled. Each time I visited her I left with a heavy heart knowing that, with no job and only a small rented field, I was unable to remove her. But I vowed that just as soon as my finances turned the corner I would bring my great horse home to the love and care she had always known.

On the evening of Thursday November 25th K— rang me to say that Bella had an infection in her foot and that she was going in for a "minor" operation. I was horrified. K— seemed completely unaware of the potential danger in anaesthetising a heavy horse: that the sheer weight can squash the tissues and squeeze the blood out of the muscles.

I spoke to his vet the next morning and after talking to Crispin gave my consent for the operation to go ahead. It didn't make me feel any better when I learned that if K— had called the vet sooner, no operation would be necessary now.

Bella survived the anaesthetic and every day I spoke to the vet for a progress report. He did not sound very optimistic.

On Friday December 5th he rang me to say that she was in great pain and my options were destruction or to put her through yet another operation which had only a 50% chance of success.

I asked Crispin's advice for the last time and then made the decision to let Bella go. She was only 10 years and eight months old.